YOUR JEWISH WEDDING

*A Complete Guide
to Arranging a Wedding,
Large or Small,
in the Unique Jewish
Tradition*

HELEN LATNER

47,272

DOUBLEDAY & COMPANY, INC.
GARDEN CITY, NEW YORK
1985

A Note on Transliterations

The transliteration system followed for Hebrew and Yiddish expressions is the one used by the Encyclopedia Judaica and the YIVO Institute (New York).

A variety of names and addresses have been used for the sake of illustration. Any similarity to those of actual people, living or dead, is unintentional.

Drawings on pp. 14 and 15 are by Abigail S. Bordeleau from The Book of Modern Jewish Etiquette *by Helen Latner, published by Schocken Books, New York. Copyright © 1981 by Helen Latner. Used by permission.*

Library of Congress Cataloging in Publication Data
Latner, Helen.
　　Your Jewish wedding.

　　1. Marriage customs and rites, Jewish.　2. Wedding
etiquette.　I. Title.
BM713.L38　1985　　　395′.22′088296
ISBN: 0-385-18873-0
Library of Congress Catalog Card Number 83–45567
Copyright © 1984, 1985 by Helen S. Latner

CONTENTS

INTRODUCTION

MAZAL TOV! You are soon to be married and you, your future husband, and your parents are all doubly blessed. When you marry, you enter what in Jewish thought is said to be the ideal state of existence, ordained since Creation. Your parents, when they lead you to the wedding canopy (the *huppah),* will be fulfilling the hope expressed in the very first blessing said over their babies—to see them as radiant bride and groom.

A complicated step, getting married, often defined by the three P's—parties, plans, and panic. What generates panic in the midst of happiness? Consider. Even the simplest wedding involves two sides of two families, at least two generations, a gamut of choices that can escalate rapidly from a no-frills ceremony at City Hall to the all-out splendor of an almost royal pageant, and a thousand and one details, most of which spell expense and/or perplexity.

The perfect wedding does not create itself. There is of necessity a great deal of preliminary planning, some of it long in advance of the day. I have written this book to help all the parties to a wedding understand the traditions that make a wedding Jewish, to point the way through the often bewildering array of choices, to suggest solutions to many problems resulting from divorces in the family, deceased parents, difference of religion, getting married in an unfamiliar community and so on, through all the little worries that will be waking you in the middle of the night, as the wedding day draws closer. Knowing what to demand and what to expect from all the people you will deal with will be an aid to working with your providers as allies, not adversaries, toward your shared goal, a beautiful, smoothly run wedding.

Weddings can be frighteningly expensive, but they need not be. I have tried to indicate ways to economize, ways to share the cost, ways to spare yourself wasted effort and exhaustion. By following this guide, you can arrange a distinctively Jewish, meaningful, and emotionally satisfying wedding, one that is not just a "package affair."

A NOTE TO THE BRIDE

Yes, it *is* your wedding and you have the right to make the final decisions, but remember, you are marrying into another family, and your bridegroom's wishes and those of his parents should at least be consulted. Parents and grandparents also have a special role in Jewish weddings; a wise bride takes these all into account in her plans. Rely on tradition and rule where you can, and put your effort into working out the details that will make your wedding special for you. The personal touches and the true rejoicing of all the family members, not the amount of money you have spent, are what will determine the lasting memories of the day.

Planning equals lists and notebooks. The more you write down, the less you have to worry about remembering. Use the questions in the checklists in this book, the pages in your guest and gift notebooks, and the countdown pages for your appointments and "do now" memos. They are designed to keep you in control and help you approach the wedding day with less confusion. You will walk down the aisle serene, radiant, and happy.

A NOTE TO THE MOTHER OF THE BRIDE

To use this book most effectively, decide together with your daughter and her fiancé on the traditions you wish to follow. Decide on your budget. This will usually determine the wedding style and the size of the guest list. Then follow the checklists and the countdown reminders together, to keep a record of all your contracts, appointments, deadlines, and expenses, and to assure that you have not forgotten anything.

A NOTE TO THE GROOM

You and your parents have a special part to play in a Jewish wedding. Chapters VII and VIII are written especially for you and your family. Share both with them and with your bride. The more you plan and prepare together, the more personally meaningful your wedding day will be.

May that day mark the beginning of a long, happy, and fruitful life together. As one says traditionally,

MAZAL TOV AND SIMAN TOV!

I

WHAT MAKES A WEDDING JEWISH?

Attitudes

Not only is the married state the ideal, it is also, in Jewish thought, a basic social institution that contributes to the advancement of society through the founding of a home and a family. Since biblical times, this "building of joy" has been observed with great festivity: music, feasting, dancing, processions, hilarity, special dress, crowns for the bride and groom, and all the joyful revelry and merrymaking the guests can devise —even tumbling, juggling, and comic versifying. It is, indeed, a special fulfillment of a commandment *(mitzvah)* to help the bride and groom rejoice on their wedding day.

On that day, in ancient times, they were regarded as a king and queen, all their wishes were granted, and the tradition arose that all their previous sins were forgiven, so that the bride and groom began their married life happily and with a "clean slate."

The wedding ceremony itself is designed to surround a legal contract publicly entered into (the *ketubbah*) with blessings that sanctify the relationship. For this reason, the ceremony is referred to as *kiddushin* (sanctification). It used to be marked with feasting for seven days (and *you* think planning for one day is bewildering!).

The entire community rejoiced and took part in the *mitzvah* of helping the couple marry and start a new household. Special care was taken to invite the poor.

For these reasons, lavish hospitality has always been a Jewish tradition. Some rabbis even gave the opinion that it was permissible to pledge or sell a Torah scroll (the most precious of holy books) to marry off a daughter. Others held that the opulence of the wedding should not be so far beyond the family's means that it became an intolerable financial burden. From the thirteenth century to today, the golden mean lies in between.

Both sets of parents and grandparents are deeply involved in a traditional ceremony, symbolizing the union of the two families. We do not "give the bride away"; rather, the parents bring their children to the wedding canopy to be consecrated to each other. Thus, they fulfill their parental duties and realize their most deeply held wishes for their children.

We hope marriages are made in heaven. There is a commentary (Midrash) that tells us that, forty days before you were born, the name of your ordained mate (your *zivuk*) is announced in heaven. And another Midrash tells us that this task of matchmaking is so important (and so arduous) that God has been occupied with it since the Creation. To arrange a match is also a *mitzvah*. No wonder everyone wanted to introduce you to "just the girl (or boy) for you!"

EXTENDED RELATIONSHIPS

A wedding creates a new degree of relationship between the two sets of parents. The word "in-laws" is used as an approximate translation of the Hebrew *mechutonim* (pl.). The mothers are each given the title *machteniste* (s.) and the fathers, *mechuton*. This relationship implies social and familial obligations which can be as close as you each choose to make them.

A good deal of pleasure can be derived from this extended family connection if both sides exercise real tact and consideration to avoid friction in the early days of planning and becoming acquainted with each other. Here the rules of etiquette help to point the way to harmony.

Making the First Visits

Let's take the formal exchange of first visits. If the two of you have just decided that this is it and you're really going to take the big step, certain courtesies must be observed. While we no longer expect the young man to ask her father formally for a woman's hand in marriage, it is still a rule of courtesy that the families should be told of your intentions to marry as soon as possible. The groom should meet her parents, and immediately afterward, he should inform his family and, if distance permits, take his bride to meet them. His mother should then call or write her mother, to tell her how happy they are to welcome her daughter into their family, and so on. The bride's mother is next expected to invite his parents to visit and that starts the mutual sharing of plans and the development of a good relationship.

Do note this—Your parents may feel just as shy about this first step as you! If your fiancé's mother hasn't made the opening move, don't wait and brood and let a breach develop. The bride's mother may always initiate the invitation herself.

If distance makes visiting difficult, use the phone and the mail to keep the communications open.

Don't forget your grandparents! Especially if they're getting on in years or live far away. They rate a special call or note from you announcing the good news, a visit to introduce the new member of the family (if distance permits), and a place in the ceremony (see Chapter II). If you tell them about their upcoming honor, you'll gladden their hearts and lengthen their years.

PREWEDDING FESTIVITIES

Everyone not only loves a bride and groom, but also seems to want to give a party for them. As your wedding day draws nearer, try to keep the partying to a minimum, to save your own energies and nerves, and to avoid burdening your wedding attendants (who will be invited to all of the showers) with the obligation to give you multiple gifts.

Some Prudent Guidelines

1. A formal engagement party is usually given only if the wedding date is about a year or more off (again, because of the burden of giving two gifts at close intervals).

2. For the same reason, shower guest lists are sometimes restricted to those who will *not* be invited to the wedding (apart from immediate family and your attendants). This allows your friends and colleagues to take part in the rejoicing.

3. Showers may not properly be given by members of the immediate family of the bride or groom.

4. Thank-you notes for shower and engagement gifts should be sent out at once. There will be many, many more to write after the wedding.

5. Announce well in advance that there are to be no parties in the last few days before the wedding, except for the groom's Torah honor *(oyfruf)* on the Sabbath before and the rehearsal party or prewedding family dinner.

If all the aunts and cousins on both sides want to host dinners in your honor and it gets to be too much, talk it over with your fiancé frankly, then ask your mothers to suggest that the relatives pool their entertaining into one or two larger family gatherings.

Setting sensible limits to the partying is a good way to insure bright eyes instead of bleary ones on the wedding day.

NOTES

II

JEWISH WEDDING TRADITIONS TO CHERISH AND HONOR

Our wedding traditions go back through history to the first betrothal and wedding mentioned in the Bible. When Rebekah, for example, first saw Isaac, her promised bridegroom, approaching her across the fields, she drew her scarf over her hair and covered her face, a Middle East custom of modesty. And so was begun the convention of veiling the bride.

The "something borrowed" tradition goes back to a practice described in the Bible: brides were customarily lent part of their wedding outfit by their friends, so that all might be more equally adorned on their wedding day.

Other time-honored usages are sometimes lost sight of as people seek to "modernize," to find offbeat, "creative" wedding styles. Many brides now return to ancient custom to arrange an authentic Jewish wedding, most "original" because it is most based on its own roots.

Your family may have its own tradition; you may wish to observe some or all of the practices described here.

JUST BEFORE THE WEDDING

Torah Honor to the Groom (the Oyfruf)

The honor to the bridegroom may begin with his being called to the Torah in synagogue on the Sabbath before the wedding. This is the occasion for a reception after services *(kiddush)* hosted by his family and is a good time for members of both families to socialize informally. In some congregations, the bridegroom is showered with nuts, raisins, and sweetmeats at the conclusion of his reading, to symbolize the wish for a sweet, fruitful life.

Mikveh and Seclusion

All converts and all traditionally observant brides go to the ritual bath (the *mikveh)* for ceremonial immersion and purification just before the wedding day. A joyful occasion, often followed by a small party for the women in the family, it also marks the seclusion of the bride, who does not see or talk to the bridegroom from then on, anywhere from a week to a day before the ceremony. At a time when your nerves are really strung out, this separation may save you from many moments of friction and tears. A sensible custom, whether you go to the *mikveh* or not!

EVENTS IN A TRADITIONAL CEREMONY

In the European village (the *shtetl*), the bridegroom and his party would arrive at the bride's village to the accompaniment of music, dancing, and merrymaking. As in Orthodox communities today, there would be separate receptions for men and women. The groom would attempt to display his learning at the festivities surrounding his signing of the marriage contract. Meantime, the bride would be feted by her women friends and relatives.

Veiling the Bride (B'deken di Kalle)

At last, when the contract formalities and celebrations are completed, the groom, escorted by his father and father-in-law in a solemn procession, comes to claim his bride. Before the joyfully singing wedding guests, he gazes at her to be sure this is the woman promised him, then lowers her face veil as the sign of a proper betrothal. Thus the groom, from time immemorial, has assured himself of avoiding the deception worked on Jacob, when he found himself married to the heavily veiled Leah instead of to Rachel, his love. A burst of joyous music from the band and rejoicing all around mark this moment of acceptance. There is a special blessing said for the bride. Now the ceremony can begin.

A moment of fervent emotion, this ritual can be added to your wedding, if you desire it in preference to your being hidden away from the guests until your first theatrical appearance as you start down the aisle. Plan for at least a half hour of reception time before the ceremony begins. Check with your caterer to be sure there is an adequate space and that the rabbi or synagogue will allow preceremony receptions (some don't). Halls and hotels that serve the Orthodox community generally have large, ornate bridal rooms.

And fear not! The bride always has *her* moment of formal assent before the groom signs the contract. From liberal Reform to the most traditionally Orthodox, the rabbi always asks the bride to state her free consent to the union. In some groups, the bride also signs the contract. This is done privately.

Wedding Canopy (Huppah)

The wedding ceremony takes place under the wedding canopy. As a reminder of the promise made to Abraham that his descendants would be as numerous as the stars in the heavens, it became a tradition to hold the ceremony out of doors, under the open sky, preferably at nightfall, when the stars could be seen. In the *shtetl,* the procession of wedding guests, carrying many candles as a sign of rejoicing, would wind its way to the village square, where the *huppah* had been set up. The entire community was witness to the event.

Today you can have your ceremony outdoors in your own garden, on the grounds of a synagogue or country club, in a city garden or park, or even on a street briefly closed to traffic for the occasion. The adventurous may consider the deck of a yacht chartered for the evening. If you think you might like one of the public areas, or a boat, start looking into permits and reservations well ahead of time. Will refreshments be permitted at the botanical gardens?

The *huppah* symbolizes the new home of the couple. In Bible days, it was a specially decorated tent set up in the courtyard of the bride's family. In time, it evolved into a velvet canopy, elaborately embroidered and fringed, and supported by four poles, which were often ornamented with garlands of flowers and greenery.

Among Sephardim, and in Israel, a large prayer shawl *(tallit)* is held over the couple as a huppah. Many couples prefer the classic simplicity of the *tallit* or the velvet canopy to the elaborate (and costly) floral arbors devised by florists. Some synagogues, in fact, do not allow a floral canopy. If you decide you really want to spend all that this fifteen-minute floral spectacle will cost, check with your synagogue before ordering it.

If you're up to it creatively, you can make your own wedding canopy, embroidered or appliquéd, which, after the wedding, will become an heirloom wall hanging.

Friends can share in the rejoicing by holding the four poles at the ceremony, or working on the embroidery with you. To be asked to participate is an honor.

Directions and designs for making your own huppah can be found in a leaflet prepared by the Women's League for Conservative Judaism and in the book, *The Work of Our Hands*, by Mae S. Rockland, published by

Schocken Books, 200 Madison Avenue, New York, NY 10016.

The Traditional Procession

The entire immediate family is customarily involved in attending the bride and groom at one of the most important events in their lives. Both bride and groom are escorted to the huppah by their mothers and fathers. If there are grandparents, they are given a special, honored place in the procession. A grandchild may be assigned to escort the very aged. All stand under the canopy, if space allows, as both witnesses and participants.

You may have as many or as few attendants as you like. Ideally, all the brothers and sisters should be part of the wedding party, but you need not have any attendants other than your parents if a simple, small wedding is your desire. A quorum *(minyan)* of ten men is usual, however, and so even a small wedding should include that number in the guest list.

A small table holding two glasses and a bottle of *kiddush* wine is set under the *huppah*. The first to enter are the rabbi and/or the cantor, who chant greetings to the couple.

The bride enters with her face veil down. It is put back during the ceremony.

The traditional order up the aisle *(Figure IA)* is:

Grandparents of the groom
(or of the bride and groom together)

Ushers (if any)

Best Man

Father, Groom, Mother (to the right of the groom)

Grandparents of the bride

Bridesmaids (if any)

Maid/Matron of Honor

Flower Girls (if any)

Father, Bride, Mother (to the right of the bride)

Under the canopy, the groom's parents take places at the right side of the rabbi, the bride's facing them at the left. Best man and maid of honor stand behind the groom and bride. Ushers and bridesmaids line the aisle. Grandparents may stand or sit on the platform beside the *huppah* or they may be seated in the first row of pews (Figure II).

See Figure IB for the order in conventional recessionals.

At Orthodox weddings, the two fathers may escort the groom; the mothers then escort the bride. In the recessional at such weddings, the two fathers follow the bride and groom, then the two mothers, then paired ushers, then paired bridesmaids. The best man leads the ushers, the maid or matron of honor leads the bridesmaids.

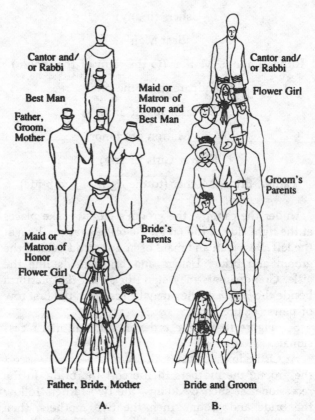

Cantor and/
or Rabbi

Best Man

Father,
Groom,
Mother

Maid or
Matron of
Honor and
Best Man

Cantor and/
or Rabbi

Flower Girl

Groom's
Parents

Bride's
Parents

Maid or
Matron of
Honor

Flower Girl

Father, Bride, Mother

Bride and Groom

A.

B.

Figure I. Up and Down the Aisle

Figure II.   Under the Huppah
*(1) Rabbi, (2) cantor, (3) groom, (4) bride, (5) groom's parents,
(6) bride's parents, (7) best man, and (8) maid of honor. Flower
girl and grandparents (if any) are seated on a side bench or in the
first row. Ushers and bridesmaids line the aisle.*

Widowed Parents

A widowed mother or father may alone escort either the bride or the groom. When the parent has remarried, the stepfather or stepmother may join in the procession or not, as personal feelings and the length of the second marriage dictate.

Divorced Parents (See Chapter XVII.)

Circling the Groom

In Orthodox custom, the bride, escorted by the two mothers (who carry lit candles, where permitted) circles the groom under the canopy before she takes her place at his right. The number of circuits varies from one to three to seven. Seven is the favorite with many because of the analogy to the seven heavens, the seven wedding blessings, and the mystical idea that the circuits symbolize the bride's entering the seven spheres of her beloved's soul. Hasidim chant a solemn melody for the circuits.

Impressive and moving, this custom is now being observed by many less traditional brides. Most rabbis will add it to the wedding ceremony if you ask. Lacking a Hasidic choir, you can have the traditional melodies played as a flute or violin solo.

Tradition-minded grandmothers and aunts will remind the bride to be sure she starts down the aisle, and on the circuits, if she does them, with her right foot. Never mind the blue garter—it's the right foot that counts!

Memorial Prayers

When a parent is deceased, custom permits special memorial prayers. More and more, these are being said privately for the families before the ceremony, but they can be inserted into the wedding service, if your feelings will permit you to regard them as honors to the departed and not as a renewal of an old grief. It is also appropriate to have these prayers said at the *oyfruf* instead of at the ceremony. Discuss this with your fiancé, your parents, and the rabbi.

The Wedding Vow and the Ring

After the introductory psalms and blessings, the groom recites the ancient Aramaic wedding vow (see Chapter VII for the text) and presents the wedding ring to his bride.

The Marriage Contract—(Ketubbah)

The *ketubbah*, a legal document spelling out the obligations and rights of both parties, is central to the wedding service, which is designed to sanctify and bless the contract. Traditionally, it is read aloud in the original Aramaic and then in English and given to the bride for safekeeping. Properly signed and witnessed, it is the Jewish equivalent of the marriage certificate and must never leave the bride's possession.

In some services, the public reading is abbreviated

to an English summary, often masked by a musical background. The full English translation is a meaningful and moving depiction of the mutual devotion entailed in marriage.

An illuminated *ketubbah* can be ordered from a calligrapher and framed to hang in your home as a cherished family document.

The Seven Wedding Blessings

The liturgy of the ceremony ends with the chanting of the seven wedding blessings, as first the groom, then the bride, sip from a cup of wine.

The reading of the blessings, in Hebrew or in English, may be divided among those male guests you wish to honor, distinguished relatives, and rabbis. The more who participate, the greater the honor to the bride and groom.

In modern, more liberal variants, women may be honored; relatives and close friends may be drawn into the ceremony.

If you want to add original readings, they would be interpolated at this point. Be sure to check with your rabbi on the procedure and the suitability of the passages you have chosen (see "Unconventional Weddings"—Chapter XIV).

Breaking the Glass

Finally, with a stamp of his right foot, the groom breaks a glass, concluding the ceremony to applause and cries of "Mazal tov!" from the guests and a burst of joyful music from the band.

The breaking of the glass, so familiar as the climax of the Jewish wedding ceremony, is done to remind us in our happiest moments of the seriousness and fragility of life. It is also taken to be a symbol of the destruction of the Temple.

The glass, a very thin, breakable one, is placed in a paper bag to avoid flying splinters. The bridegroom should be careful to step squarely on the packet with the instep and heel of his foot to be sure of breaking the glass at the first blow. Tell your caterer you do *not* want him to use a flashbulb in the bag, as some do. Though it makes a very loud noise when broken, the practice is vulgar and produces ribald laughter among the guests. Do you want that at your wedding?

Union (Yihud)

The groom's recitation of the wedding vow and gift of the ring to the bride, and the reading of the *ketubbah* are two of the three legal elements of a Jewish ceremony; the third is the symbolic consummation of the marriage in the ritual known as union *(yihud)*. After the joyous recessional, when they proceed down the aisle together as man and wife, the bride and groom immediately retire for a brief time to a private room where they partake of some food together, usually a rich, golden "wedding broth."

When the *yihud* custom is followed, the bride and groom make a formal entrance to their reception after this brief interval, to a triumphant fanfare from the band. There is no receiving line.

The Traditional Ring

A traditionally correct wedding ring, usually gold, may not be pierced (carved) or set with stones, because, according to Jewish law, it must be an object of readily apparent value, the acceptance of which signifies the bride's full consent to the contract. Carving could lessen the gold weight, stones might be false or of uncertain value, thus deceiving the bride.

Modern brides may want to use the plain band for the ceremony and don a more elaborate ring afterward.

During the ceremony, the ring is first placed on the right forefinger of the bride. That is considered the finger of the intelligence because it is the one we use to point out the letters when reading the Torah. The ring may be moved to the conventional ring finger of the left hand after the ceremony.

Double-ring ceremonies are not traditional, but may be allowed in more liberal congregations.

Your ring can be engraved inside, reading: groom's initials/to/bride's initials/date. Reverse the order for the groom's ring.

Traditional Dancing

Circle dancing to lively Hasidic and Israeli tunes is an essential part of the rejoicing. Even the most staid of wedding receptions comes alive when the first notes of this traditional music sound. The climax is reached when the bride and groom, queen and king of the day, are raised aloft in chairs in the center of a whirling circle.

Among the Orthodox, men and women do not dance together; however, the bride may dance with her father or father-in-law or other older male relatives by holding the end of a kerchief stretched between them. This picturesque custom (the *mitzvah-tants)* is often followed even at a reception where mixed dancing is permitted.

When either the bride or the groom is the last child of a family to be married, a special dance, the *mazinkeh-tants,* is done for the parents. They are seated in the center of the circle and sometimes presented with wreaths to wear. All sing and dance in their honor, a special recognition of the "empty nest" and the accomplishment of a classic Jewish goal—marrying off all one's children.

APPROPRIATE MUSIC FOR A JEWISH WEDDING

Brides of every faith are beginning to avoid using the march from *Lohengrin* by Wagner (popularly known as "Here Comes the Bride") and the Mendelssohn recessional as too cliché. For a Jewish wedding, this music is particularly inappropriate; one (the *Lohengrin)* was written to celebrate a mystical Christian union (never consummated!) and the other to grace a pagan wedding. One is by a notorious anti-Semite, the other by an apostate Jew.

A choice of more original and authentically Jewish music may be made from among the many Hasidic,

Yiddish folk and Israeli melodies used at traditional weddings. In addition, there are specially composed wedding services commissioned and published by the Union of American Hebrew Congregations (Reform) and the New York City Cantors Assembly (Conservative). The traditional and Hasidic music is beginning to be published in book form and may be found at Jewish bookstores.

Your cantor, rabbi, or the choir director are also good sources of distinctive musical settings for your wedding. The Women's League for Conservative Judaism (48 East 74th Street, New York) publishes a pamphlet, "Music to Wed By," that lists many compositions and gives sources for sheet music. There is a nominal charge for this publication.

Classical music played by a trio, a flutist, or the organist is also a suitable and original choice in place of the wedding "Evergreens" for the procession.

If you give your musicians the sheet music well ahead of time, they will be happy to learn it and perform it for you. So, unless you have your heart set on going down the aisle to the "good, old reliable" strains of the wedding march, don't use it just because everyone else has.

CHARITY (TZEDAKAH)

In a time of rejoicing, we are instructed to remember the poor, the lonely, and the sick. Both families may make a charitable donation and some guests often make a gift in the name of the couple to an organization they favor.

In the same spirit, some families give the floral centerpieces and other decorations to hospitals or senior citizens' homes after the reception. If this is not done, it is also in the tradition of generosity to arrange some orderly system of giving the table flowers to the guests to take home. Discuss it with the caterer and have the master of ceremonies announce whatever disposition of the flowers you have decided on.

Also see "After the Wedding" (Chapter XIX) for a note on donating your wedding gown to a charity in Israel so that poor brides may use it.

NOTES

III

WHEN, WHERE, AND HOW

WHEN—CHOOSING A DATE

Before you set a date for your wedding, you must take into account certain times when marriages may not be performed.

Weddings are not permitted (in all groups) on:

> the Sabbath (Friday evening to Saturday after sundown)
>
> the major holidays (Rosh Hashanah, Yom Kippur, Passover, Shavout and Sukkot—sundown to sundown)

Orthodox and Conservative congregations also exclude:

> the Three Weeks (the period between the 17th of Tammuz and the 9th of Av—usually during July and August)
>
> the *Sefirah* period (the seven weeks between Passover and Shavout, except for Lag b'Omer—usually in April and May)

These times are held to be periods of national mourning.

Sephardic and Reform practice:

Sephardim allow marriages during Sefirah from Lag b'Omer on.

Reform groups allow marriages during both these periods, except for the 9th of Av.

How can you check the exact calendar dates of these days? Get yourself a Hebrew calendar (a *Luach),* which sets forth all the major and minor Jewish holidays, gives candle-lighting time, and much other useful information. You can get one either in the form of an appointment diary or a wall calendar from any of the major Jewish organizations, or your synagogue. The year starts at Rosh Hashanah (September) in these calendars. You will find it helpful also in selecting other party dates that will not pose problems for observant guests.

Mourning

Weddings may not take place during the thirty days of mourning observed for a brother or sister or the eleven-month period for a parent. Reform congregations keep the thirty-day rule for all periods of mourning.

A wedding may not be postponed, once the date is set, however, even if there is a death in the family, since not even mourning is permitted to interfere with a wedding, the highest of *mitzvot.* Usually, however, the music is eliminated in these circumstances and the whole scale of the reception reduced.

How Much "Lead Time" Do You Need?

For the most fashionable synagogues and hotels and the most popular times (Saturday nights, holiday weekends, Sunday noon), reservations may be necessary six months to a year in advance.

The minimum time, if you intend to observe any formality at all, is three months. Caterers, florists, musicians, and photographers all require advance notice. Formal invitations must be sent out at least four weeks before the date. Delivery of custom-fitted dresses, engraved wedding rings, personalized favors, and the like takes at least four weeks as well, not to mention the shopping time involved.

It is possible to arrange a small, informal wedding in a short time, but leaving yourself less than a month will create an almost intolerable pressure that makes for frenzied arrangements, neglected details, frazzled nerves, and family friction.

Allow yourself enough time, if you can, to set a sensible pace. Whatever the time at your disposal, follow the checklists so that you can relax and savor all the anticipatory excitement and the wedding itself.

CONFERRING WITH THE RABBI

The rabbi who officiates will want to meet with you and the groom to ascertain that the wedding may properly take place under Jewish law and to obtain information for the preparation of the *ketubbah*.

You will need to know your Hebrew name and your

parents' Hebrew names. If either of the parties (and in some Orthodox groups, the parents) were divorced, Orthodox and Conservative rabbis require proof that a religious divorce decree (a *get*) was granted. Reform groups accept a civil divorce decree.

Problems arising from divorce can be resolved, but they take time. If this is your situation, see the officiating rabbi as soon as you set the date; do not wait until a week or two before the wedding.

If there will be a sermon, the rabbi or officiant will seek enough information, if he does not already know you, to enable him to make some appropriate personal remarks.

You should also have a conference shortly before the wedding with the sexton *(shammash)* or the ritual director, to discuss the procedures governing picture-taking, floral decorations, the music for the ceremony, and the rehearsal plans. By this time, you should have decided what special rituals you want included in the ceremony.

Be sure to ask (if you want these observances):

> Can we have a double-ring ceremony?
>   circuits of the groom?
>   special readings?
>   special music?

Also ask exactly what the ceremony ritual will be.

Take nothing for granted if you are unfamiliar with the procedures of the synagogue or club. Especially when the caterer provides the officiant, assure yourself that the ritual meets with your approval and is traditionally correct. You may ask to observe the next wedding there, if you wish.

WHERE TO HOLD THE WEDDING

Though a Jewish wedding need not be held in a synagogue, the most dignified and impressive place for a wedding is the sanctuary, if the size of your wedding party permits. Most large synagogues have an official caterer who can supervise all the reception details for you, and a ritual director who will assure the correctness of the religious procedure.

Even if there is no caterer, or your party is too large or too small for the reception space available, consider having the ceremony in the sanctuary (main *shul)* or the small chapel, and the reception elsewhere.

The Possibilities

In order of formality and cost, wedding locales rank approximately:

1. fashionable synagogue, club, or hotel on Saturday night, Sunday, or eves of legal holidays

2. same—weeknights

3. catering halls—Saturday nights and Sundays are more expensive than weeknights

4. restaurants or clubs—can be combined with synagogue

5. home—yours or a friend's, fully catered

6. champagne or cocktail reception at home or in an elegant restaurant

Note: Weeknight weddings may start as early as 6 P.M. and consequently end earlier. Tuesday is often chosen by the observant, because, as we read in Genesis, on that day God twice "saw that it was good."

A wedding ceremony on Saturday may not be held until about one hour after sundown. In the spring and summer, sundown is so late that the festivities may run well past midnight, incurring overtime fees for musicians and catering services.

When considering these possibilities, the number of guests is also a deciding factor. If your party is small (under forty), most institution caterers are not willing to consider it at all, because their base cost is so high. They also often reserve the most sought-after dates for the largest wedding parties. Obviously, 250 people in the main ballroom will bring in much more revenue than one hundred. A small party must perforce be held in a restaurant, a private room at a hotel or club, or at home.

To shop sensibly for a place to hold your reception, do a preliminary head count. Assume that about one fourth of the people on the list will not be able to attend (more, if many are from out of town). That estimate will indicate to you what size of reception hall you need to look for.

The Home Wedding

A home wedding can be warmly personal, informal, and yet memorable. It can also be a stressful effort unless family and friends really give substantial help or a reliable caterer takes over.

Using outside help and rented equipment can make

your wedding at home almost as costly as one catered in a hotel or synagogue, especially as the number of guests rises and luxurious details are added. The size of your guest list, the degree of formality and the atmosphere you desire to create, and the balance of cost against convenience and sentiment will all be factors in your decision. If you have always wanted to be married on a June day in your family's garden, or in front of the fireplace in the living room, give careful consideration to all the questions below before you make up your mind.

Checklist for a Home Wedding

Consider:

1. What ambiance are you seeking?

2. Will your house and garden require extensive refurbishing?

                         Approximate cost $_____

3. If the party is planned for outdoors, is there adequate indoor space, if it should rain (horrid thought)?

4. Is there room (and budget) for music and dancing? $_____

5. Is there sufficient space for
        buffet tables
        seating guests
        coats

bathroom needs
food preparation and serving
privacy for the bride before
   the ceremony

6. Who will supply the food and drink?

Approximate cost $_____

7. How much help will you require to serve and clean up?

Approximate cost $_____

8. How much rented furniture and tableware will you need?

$_____

9. Who will be assigned to the house on the wedding day, while you are at the synagogue, or out in the garden, to answer the phone, the doorbell, tidy up the bathrooms, and oversee the coat storage?

$_____

10. Can you obtain the services of a professional "host" or "hostess" to see that the events of the wedding move along as planned, and that guests are comfortable and happy?

$_____

11. Will you need special police (or parking attendants) to control traffic at the house or the special location you have chosen?

$_____

After working out the approximate cost, add at least half again to allow for unforeseen contingencies (for example, sales tax on all the food, drink, and rentals, or sharp price increases), then compare the total with the cost of one outside caterer, at least, before you reach a decision.

If you seek a homelike atmosphere, you may be able to find a caterer who can provide a rented brownstone or mansion for the day. For a small party, the hospitality suite of a fine hotel is also an elegant, homelike choice.

WHEN THERE IS A DIFFERENCE OF RELIGION

If the non-Jewish partner decides to undergo conversion, be sure to allow time for the necessary instruction and formalities—a twelve- to sixteen-week conversion course in Reform practice, much longer in Conservative groups.

No Orthodox or Conservative rabbi will perform a ceremony if one partner is not Jewish; only a few Reform rabbis will do so, usually on the promise to keep a Jewish home and raise the children in the Jewish faith.

When this is not possible, a tactful solution is to have a civil ceremony performed by an Ethical Culture minister, a justice of the peace, or a judge. The ceremony can be very moving and dignified without mention of specific religious doctrine. You may have any reception you desire after a civil ceremony.

AFTER AN ELOPEMENT

Have you and your fiancé, for whatever reason, run off impulsively to be married in a civil ceremony that shortcuts all the festivities? You may find that your parents insist on a traditional *huppah*.

They are not being unreasonably conventional. To the tradition-minded, a wedding between two Jewish partners is not complete (in the religious sense) until it has been sanctified by the religious vows and blessings. These feelings can be very strong even in people who are not especially observant in their daily practice.

Be gracious and loving toward your parents. Give them this gratification of their good wishes for you by going through the religious ceremony with good grace and by rejoicing with them at a reception. Even though you have already gone through the civil formalities, the religious rite may very appropriately be performed afterward. In some foreign countries, it is customary to separate the civil and religious ceremonies in just this way. If getting married is good, reaffirming that vow under the traditional *huppah* must be even better!

The invitations may be issued to "a reception honoring the marriage" if the ceremony will be private, or you may use the usual form. The ceremony is unchanged. The reception is the same in every respect.

HOW—WHAT STYLE FOR YOU?

Discuss with your fiancé the wedding style you two would really prefer. If simplicity is your choice, resist escalating ideas from parents—*but* remember they have long looked forward to rejoicing with all the relatives, and their friends and yours. Don't squabble over the big moment they are awaiting, that walk down the aisle, with you, their son or daughter, between them.

If you plan an elaborate wedding, keep your family finances in mind. No family should go deeply into debt to arrange a wedding that is obviously far beyond their means, just as no family should have the splashiest, most extravagant wedding they can devise just because they can afford it. By discarding unnecessary frills and sensibly limiting the guest list, you should be able to settle on a choice agreeable to all.

Checklist

Consider these costly frills:

	Cost	Total
Do you need or want a floral *huppah*?	$_____	
full floral decorations in the synagogue?	_____	
white glove "French" service?	_____	
rolling bar cart through dinner?	_____	

full smorgasbord buffet
just before dinner? ⎯⎯⎯⎯⎯

Viennese table after
dinner? ⎯⎯⎯⎯⎯

desserts *and* a wedding
cake? ⎯⎯⎯⎯⎯

wedding favors other
than skullcaps *(yarmulkes)?* $⎯⎯⎯　　$⎯⎯⎯

	Number	Total
Shall you invite		
people who do not know the bride and groom?	⎯⎯⎯	
relatives you haven't seen in years?	⎯⎯⎯	
parents' business connections?	⎯⎯⎯	
professional colleagues?	⎯⎯⎯	⎯⎯⎯

You can prune the guest list by eliminating some of these categories. Or, you can cut costs by inviting some guests to a buffet reception only, before a smaller dinner for family and close friends. Some collation must be offered to all who attend.

IV

WEDDING COSTS

SHARING EXPENSES

In the conventional division of wedding expenses, the bride's family, as hosts, pays most of the costs. Families sometimes decide to share the costs, especially when the guest list is very large, or the groom's family is much larger than the bride's.

The groom's family should initiate any suggestions as to sharing expenses during the preliminary discussion of the wedding plans. A decision should be made at the outset, before any plans are set, to eliminate friction later on.

The bride's family decides on the budget and the type of wedding. However, custom decrees that they may not demand that the groom's family contribute, and his family, in turn, may not ask for a more lavish reception style than that proposed. Any offer the groom's family makes to share must be done tactfully, never implying that one family is not generous enough or not able to live up to the hospitality standard of the other.

WHO PAYS FOR WHAT (CONVENTIONAL ARRANGEMENTS)

The Bride or Her Family Pay for:

the bridal gown and veil

the bride's trousseau

the household trousseau

invitations and announcements, addressing and postage

rental fee for synagogue or hall and all incidental rentals

fees to sexton, organist, and any other music for the ceremony

floral decorations

* bouquets and corsages for the bridal party (bride, bridesmaids, grandmother, father's boutonniere)

gifts to bridesmaids

transportation of bridal party to synagogue and reception

tips for special duty police or parking and

The Groom or His Family Pay for:

the engagement and wedding rings

fees for marriage license

fees for rabbi and/or cantor (if not included in the synagogue fee)

* corsages for his mother and grandmother and boutonnieres for himself, his father, and the ushers

the groom's wedding clothes

gifts to ushers

* groom's gift to the bride

charitable gift (tzedakah) in honor of the couple

the honeymoon

the new home and most of its major furnishings

   cloakroom attendants
* all costs for the reception, including music
* wedding pictures
  wedding ring for groom
    (if used)
  charitable gift *(tzedakah)*
    in honor of the couple
* bride's gift to the
  groom

* See the discussion following of these starred items.

COSTS THAT MAY BE SHARED

Flowers

Most grooms now treat the flowers for the bridal party, especially the bride's bouquet, as a gift to the bride. They may pay for the bridesmaids' bouquets or these may be regarded as part of the floral decorations and, therefore, the bride's responsibility.

Wedding Pictures

The bride's family plans and pays for the photos, but it is gracious to ask the groom's family what photos they would like taken. They pay for any prints they order for themselves. Sometimes the cost of albums for both families and the couple is shared equally by both.

Wines and Liquors

Many grooms offer to provide the champagne (traditional for weddings) and the other wines and liquors to be served, as their contribution to the celebration.

Sharing per Invitation

When the caterer gives a per person price for the reception, the groom's family may offer to pay for some or all of their guests. This is more equitable when his family is much larger than hers.

The groom's primary responsibility is for the costs in his list. His family may decide to offer no additional contribution because of the high cost of fitting out a new home and a professional office (if needed), and the wedding trip.

A mature and financially independent bride and groom arranging their own wedding often agree to share the cost evenly between them.

WEDDING DAY GIFTS

Bride and groom exchange gifts on the wedding day, usually a piece of jewelry (perhaps a family heirloom) that will be a permanent keepsake of the occasion.

Parents may also make a gift of personal jewelry to their new son- or daughter-in-law.

The wedding itself is a gift from the parents to their children.

A NEW ATTITUDE TOWARD SHARING THE COST OF A WEDDING

Consider this paragraph from a bulletin on weddings issued by the Women's League for Conservative Judaism:

Wedding expenses should be equally divided by the families of both bride and groom. Why should it be only the parents of the bride who have to be burdened with an often huge expense? (And if the groom's parents are of much greater means, let them accept a greater financial burden.) This would solve the 'number of guests allotted' dilemma, plus so many other problems that come up 'because I am making the wedding.' In this way, both families would have the joy of actual involvement in the planning of the wedding.

NOTES

V

THE
GUEST LIST

WHOM TO INVITE

Decide, in conference with your fiancé and his family, how large your guest list will be. For a preliminary rough estimate, count in all family members of the bride and groom, close friends of both families, long-time business associates and professional colleagues, and perhaps even neighbors and family servants. The rabbi and cantor (and their wives) are also invited to the reception, unless you do not know them at all. At a large formal affair, some people invite many more than they expect will attend, letting the invitation serve as an announcement. Experience shows that "regrets" come to about 25 percent of those invited from a large list.

It is customary to allow the groom's family half of the invitations.

In Jewish tradition, no one is invited only to the

ceremony. All guests are served some refreshments and wine at the very least, to wish a long and happy life to the newlyweds (to "make a *lechayim"*).

What can you do if the list balloons out into a much larger party than you want or can afford? One good rule of thumb for limiting the invitations is not to invite anyone who does not know either the bride or the groom personally. Another is to evaluate distant family connections objectively. If you have not seen certain relatives or heard from them in many years, perhaps you can send them an announcement instead of an invitation. In very large families, some hosts invite only one cousin from each branch, as the representative of the family. But beware—excluding some relatives has been known to create family feuds.

Children are usually not invited to a formal wedding, especially if it will be held in the evening. If you make exceptions for child attendants, you may make enemies of those who were asked to leave their children home.

Children are easier to cope with at a small, informal wedding, but if you have decided not to have them, be firm about it, should people call and ask whether they may bring their little darlings.

If you do include children, it may make life easier for all if you can provide a baby-sitter or two for the very youngest, so that their parents can enjoy the party and still feel that the youngsters are under control.

ORGANIZING THE GUEST LIST

Organizing your guest list efficiently is an important first step. Properly set up, it will help you keep track of acceptances, gifts, and thank-you notes, and become a useful family directory after the wedding.

You will be combining the lists of two families. Set a date, at least eight weeks ahead, for your fiancé to give you his family's list, with full names, addresses with zip codes, phone numbers, and some notation as to relationship. (Is Mr. XY an uncle or a business partner?)

At the same time, assemble your own list, making the same notations.

Now comes the organizing step. It may seem like a chore, but it is an essential factor in keeping calm and organized during the coming weeks.

You may set up a card file, as some experts suggest, or make up a "bride's book." In my experience, for lists up to one hundred names (about two hundred guests), the book is more versatile and easier to use than a card file. After the wedding there will be one slim notebook to keep, instead of a cumbersome file box. And you will want to use it many times—my own book, with additions, was used for the birth announcements of my four children and served as a base for my children's bar and bat mitzvah books.

Whichever system you choose, organize the list by dividing the names into three categories:

Bride's family: relatives
                  parents' friends
                  my friends
Groom's family: relatives
                  parents' friends
                  his friends

Our mutual friends and associates

If the lists are not long, you may merge them into alphabetical order and note who's who in the entries you are going to make next.

Each family should also prepare a similar list of those who are to receive announcements only.

The Card File

Next, for a card file, write up a separate index card for each complete name and address, alphabetize each category and arrange them in a good-looking file box, behind alphabet dividers. Make appropriate category notes on each card, just in case they should get scrambled when you are working with them later.

Use another set of dividers for the "announcement only" list.

The Bride's Book

To make a bride's book, purchase a nicely bound notebook, alphabet tabs, and dividers. Head each section and large divider with the category, then enter the names and addresses in a column down the left half of the page. Rule columns down the remaining width of the page for the following notations: Accept or Regret

(A/R), Gift, Thank-you Note (N). Make a separate section for the announcement list. If you prefer a small notebook, use the facing right-hand page for the notations.

The Divided List

Are you planning a function where some guests will be invited to the ceremony and reception only, and others to the dinner or luncheon following? In your card file, you may use either different colored cards or colored markers to flag this. In your bride's book, you should add another column for the notations "R" (invited to reception only), or "D" (reception and dinner).

Checklist for Addresses

As you write up your entries, check for "missing parts":

Do you have *full* names: first, last, no abbreviations?
Are titles (Dr., Senator, Rabbi, etc.) indicated?
Do you have all the zip codes? Missing numbers can be found in the post office Zip Code Directory.
Do you have phone numbers for as many as possible?

Let's hope no one is discourteous enough not to respond, but you may need to phone some of them, alas, as the reply deadline nears. Should there be some last minute change in your plans, the listed phone numbers will help cut down on the confusion.

Keeping the list in order and addressing and mailing invitations and announcements is the responsibility of the bride and her mother, but you can easily share this duty with your fiancé and work together on the details.

In your bride's book, you can also add a separate section to make a permanent record of the names, addresses, and phone numbers of the service suppliers you've jotted down in your note pages, with comments on their work. It's also interesting to keep the menu, with comments on the food. You won't forget then that the Baked Alaska was a delight, or the Chinese tidbits a disaster, when it's time to plan another party.

A TYPICAL PAGE IN A BRIDE'S BOOK

BRIDE'S FAMILY

Name and Address	R/D	A/R	Gift	N
Mr. and Mrs. Charles Green 201 West Chestnut Street Chicago, IL 60610 312/864-8084	D	A	Cut Glass Bowl	11/17/83
Mr. and Mrs. Edward Schwarz 350 Central Park West New York, NY 10025 212/423-9087	D	R	—	—

VI

INVITATIONS AND ANNOUNCEMENTS

To be invited to a wedding is an honor, and so some families send invitations to everyone on their lists, even when they live far away and will obviously not be able to attend. The invitation then serves also as an announcement.

Formal wedding announcements are optional and are sent only to those who were not invited to the wedding. You order them at the same time as the invitations, in the same typestyle. You send them out the day after the wedding, never before.

Invitations can run the gamut from handwritten informal notes for a small wedding to completely formal engraved folders for a large function.

Order your invitations as soon as you have an estimate of the number of guests, at least two months ahead, since they should be mailed out at least four weeks before the date. For June or holiday weekend weddings, six weeks' notice to your guests is even better. Don't forget to count into your totals extra invitations and announcements as keepsakes for your parents and yourselves.

Ask to pick up the envelopes early, and order some extra to allow for mistakes made while addressing them. This will enable you to start the addressing while the printing is still being done.

A fine stationer can be very helpful in showing you samples of elegant style and suggesting correct wording for varying family situations. However, many are not fully conversant with established Jewish tradition. Knowing what to ask for will help you select a stationer who can produce your invitation as you want it made, within the bounds of invitation conventions.

WORDING THE INVITATION

Traditional Formal Style

The traditional Jewish wedding invitation is written in Hebrew and English. The names of both families appear as sponsors of the wedding.

The Hebrew text is a set form, incorporating many blessings. It may be hand-lettered for you, with many traditional embellishments by a Hebrew scribe *(sofer)* or a calligrapher, or set up in type, if Hebrew typesetting is available.

You can locate the craftsmen who do such work through a Hebrew bookstore in your area, or in the advertising pages of Jewish newspapers. In many cities, calligraphers may be listed in the yellow pages of the phone book.

The English text combines the Hebrew tradition with a variant form of the usual formal wording. It may read either:

Mr. and Mrs. David Gold	(her parents)
and	
Mr. and Mrs. Joseph Levy	(his parents)
request the honour of your presence	(note "honour")
at the marriage of their children	
Rachel	
and	(note "and")
Jonathan	

or:

Mr. and Mrs. David Gold	
request the honour of your presence	
at the marriage of their daughter	
Rachel	
to	(note "to")
Dr. Jonathan Levy	
son of Mr. and Mrs. Joseph Levy	
on etc.	

When Hebrew and English are used, you may place the two texts on facing inside pages of the folder, or on consecutive pages. Which comes first? You may decide for yourself. If the English is to come first, have that printed on page one and the Hebrew on page three, so that the folder opens from right to left, in the usual book order. If the Hebrew is to come first, reverse the order, with the Hebrew on page four, and the English on page two, so that the folder opens from left to right (Hebrew book order).

An ornamental cover design, incorporating a Hebrew text and the first names of the bride and groom, may be used on page one of a folder where the texts go side by side on pages two and three, or on the overleaf of a large invitation designed to be folded in half again before inserting it in the envelope.

If there will be a traditional preceremony reception for the groom and the bride, the time of the ceremony is sometimes added after the announced assembly time in a line reading, "Huppah at _____ o'clock."

Conventional Formal Invitations

In conventional formal style, only the names of the bride's parents appear as hosts; the names of the groom's parents do not appear. If your fiancé's family want their names on the invitation, even though a Hebrew page is not being used, you may follow Jewish tradition by using either one of the forms shown for the two-language invitation.

The line "request the honour of your presence" is used for ceremonies held in a synagogue. When the wedding is held at home, in a hotel or club, this line would read "request the pleasure of your company."

If all the guests will be invited to the entire function, no separate reception card is needed. The line "and afterward at the reception" is inserted between the name of the synagogue or hotel and the address, when the ceremony and reception take place in one location.

Reception or dinner cards are needed only if you are dividing your guest list, or the text is too long to combine the invitations. These cards are printed in the same typeface and on the same stock as the invitation, but no envelope is used.

Reply cards, once frowned upon, are now widely used instead of an R.S.V.P. line, as giving maximum convenience to host and guest alike.

A deadline date is given (usually two weeks before the date) and a stamped envelope, imprinted with the host's name and address, is enclosed with the card.

Variations on the Formal Text

A less formal invitation may have second and third lines reading "invite you to share in the joy/of the wedding uniting their children" or "invite you to join in the celebration/of the marriage of their children/Barbara and Paul" (note the use of "and" in this form). The names of both families appear as hosts.

Paper and Ink

How original do you want to be? Purists feel that only engraving or thermography on off-white or ivory papers in black ink is correct for a formal invitation. In slightly less formal styles, there are infinite variations of colored inks and papers from which to choose. Extras like colored envelope linings, oversize bordered cards, metallic inks, and special monograms run up the costs. Is matching ink available for addressing envelopes? Will the large size cost more to mail? You will want to consider all these factors before making your final choice.

Informal Invitations

Formal engraved invitations are not necessary for a small wedding, or one that will be held on short notice. Handwritten notes, in the name of your mother or both your parents as hosts, may be sent instead.

You might write a note that reads:

Dear Mildred and Jack:

Our daughter Sarah will be married to Gabriel Davis here at our home on Sunday, March 12, at twelve noon. We (or David and I) *would be delighted to have you join us at this joyful ceremony and the luncheon immediately following.*

Cordially yours,
Helen and David
(or Helen)

R.S.V.P.
12 Meadow Lane
Fairlawn, N.J.

Note: You need sign your family name only if the guest is not an intimate acquaintance or close relative.

If you need more letters than you can conveniently write, you can make up a specially worded informal note and have it offset from a handwritten or calligrapher's copy on an art folder. Check to be sure you can get the right size matching envelopes before you have the notes printed.

If time is short, you may give your phone number for the R.S.V.P. Who will answer the phone? Be sure you have your list alongside the phone so the responses can be accurately checked off.

NAME PROBLEMS

When:	*Use as Name of Host(s)*	*"At the Marriage of"*
divorced parents host together	Mrs. Annabel Silver Mr. Harold Silver (separate lines—no "and")	their daughter Jennifer
divorcée hosts by herself	Mrs. Annabel Silver	*her* daughter Jennifer
divorcée has resumed own name	Ms. Annabel Loewy	*her* daughter Jennifer Silver*
When the host is: a widow	Mrs. Philip Marcus	her daughter Barbara
a widower	Mr. Philip Marcus	*his* daughter Barbara
a remarried mother	Mr. and Mrs. David Rose or Evelyn and David Rose	*her* daughter Abigail Stern*

| a remarried father | Mr. and Mrs. Joseph Stone | *his* daughter Natalie |
| a relative not the bride's parent | Mr. and Mrs. Arthur Davis | their sister (or granddaughter) Marian Gordon* |

* Note: The bride's surname is given because it is different from the name of the host(s).

A deceased parent is not mentioned in an invitation, though the name may appear in newspaper announcements.

The Bride's Own Invitation

The bride may send invitations in her own name if she lives independently or has no close relatives who are acting as hosts.

The formal wording is:

The honour of your presence

is requested at the marriage of

Dr. Elizabeth Schneider

to (or "and")

Mr. Solomon Wise

etc.

The Couple's Own Invitation

When a couple are hosting their own wedding, they may use the same form, or make up an informal invitation inviting the guests to "our wedding" and signed with both their names.

THE POST OFFICE FORMALITIES

Return Addresses

Post office regulations require a return address. Though, theoretically, this should be in the front upper-left corner of the envelope, the post office, I was assured, will not refuse your mail if you put the return address on the back flap.

You may use an embossed return address. You can order a die and have the stationer do it for you, or save money by buying your own embosser and doing it yourself.

Transparent calligraphy-style labels, the self-sticking kind, are an attractive alternative. Be sure you have left enough time for your label order to be completed and delivered to you, whichever style of return address you choose.

Proper Postage

Your letter will not be delivered if you do not put sufficient postage on it. Assemble the invitation and its enclosures. Have it weighed at the post office. A maxi-

mum thickness of 1/4 inch and a maximum size of
6 1/8" by 11 1/2" is allowed on the base postal rate for
one ounce or less. Some invitations, when fully assem-
bled, become oversize letters which require additional
postage. How much postage do you need? Are you
sending many invitations overseas? Check the rate for
airmail to those destinations.

An appropriate commemorative stamp adds a distinctive touch to an elegant invitation. Take the time
to select one at the philately window and order it
ahead, if you need more than your post office has on
hand at one time.

ADDRESSING INVITATIONS

Before you begin the work of addressing your invitations, run down this checklist:

Did you order enough invitations (including keepsake copies)?

Is your address list in order?

Did you pick up *all* the envelopes (extras in case of
mistakes and *two* sets—glued ones for the mailing envelope, unglued ones for the inside envelope)?

Do you have

     matching ink for addressing?
     extra pens so friends can help?
     return address labels or an embosser?
     stamps—for reply envelopes and for mailing?
     a moistener for stamps and flaps?
     enclosure with travel directions, if needed?

Now you are ready to begin. If you have decided to have the envelopes addressed by a professional calligrapher, the finishing touch for an elegant invitation, you are now ready to turn over your address list, return labels, invitations and stamps, and have the whole job done for you. A pleasant little luxury!

If you are doing it yourself, you can have your fiancé or your friends or bridesmaids help. A cheerful assembly line for folding, inserting, labeling or embossing, and sealing and affixing stamps makes the addressing chore go faster—and it's lots more fun!

ADDRESSING PROTOCOL

1. Send a separate invitation to every adult couple and single person on your list, also, every family member over eighteen still living at home. All the grown sisters and brothers may receive one joint invitation.

2. All addresses must be handwritten, *never* typed, or, perish the thought, on computer labels. Use black ink or a color that matches the text.

3. No abbreviations are used, except for Mr., Mrs., Ms., Dr., and Jr. Use initials only if you cannot ascertain the full name.

4. The word "and" is spelled out.

5. A correctly addressed mailing envelope will look like this:

Dr. and Mrs. Martin Goldsmith
1400 Chestnut Street
Philadelphia, Pennsylvania Zip

Note the preferred indented form, which is very elegant on a large envelope. Block form is also correct.

6. The expression "and family" is not used.

7. The inside envelope carries only the surname, centered as

Dr. and Mrs. Goldsmith

THE RIGHT TITLE—INSCRIBING ENVELOPES

Name Situation	*Outside Envelope**	*Inside Envelope†*
Mr. and Mrs.	full names	Dr. and Mrs. Goldsmith
young children	no "and family"— children are included on inside address	Dr. and Mrs. Goldsmith Jonathan and Eliza
family members over 18		
two sisters	The Misses (or Misses) Jane and Alice Grant (one line)	The Misses Grant
two brothers	The Messrs. (or Messrs.) Paul and Benjamin Grant (one line)	The Messrs. Grant

a brother and a sister	Mr. Benjamin and Miss Alice Grant (one line)	Mr. and Miss Grant
live-togethers	list names in alphabetical order, one under the other Miss (or Ms.) Grace Ross Mr. Edward Taylor	Ms. Ross Mr. Taylor (no "and")
married woman using own name	Mr. Stephen Black and Ms. Helen Weiss (both names on one line, joined by "and")	Mr. Black and Ms. Weiss
a widow	Mrs. Aaron Davis	Mrs. Davis
a divorcée	Ms. (or Mrs.) Pauline Gold	Ms. (or Mrs.) Gold
two doctors	Drs. Paul and Edna Bloom	The Doctors Bloom

* Full address goes under the title in each case, following the example on page 60.
† Title and surname only, as shown here.

ASSEMBLING INVITATIONS

You will receive your invitations flat, but scored for folding, with a pack of tissues to place over the type. Fold the invitations along the score line with the text side out, except where facing Hebrew and English pages are used.

For the smaller sizes, now place a protective tissue on top of the text, or between the two pages. Insert the invitations in the inner envelope with the fold up, and the text side facing up as one opens the flap.

Fold large-size folders in half once more, with a half tissue between, then insert with the fold up.

If there are enclosure cards, place them on top of the tissue-covered text in the smaller size, or inside the fold in the larger size, with the type facing the same way.

If you use reply cards, the envelopes for the cards must be stamped for first-class mail. The card is not inserted in the envelope, but placed under its flap, ready for use.

Now close the inner envelope and put it inside the outer envelope, inscribed side up as one opens the flap.

Double-check the weight of the whole set for first-class postage.

Save yourself time and confusion at the post office by dividing the finished invitations at home into local, out-of-town, and foreign mail. Keep the foreign mail separate and make sure the postage is correct.

If your reply cards were delivered in a box by the printer, keep the box. You can drop the cards in as they return to you, sort them out alphabetically, and check them off quickly as they come in. When the time comes to count them and to make up your seating chart, you will have them all together.

ADDRESSING ANNOUNCEMENTS

Announcements are addressed in the same manner as invitations. Since there is only one envelope, there is no inner address to worry about. Insert the announcement card with the fold up, type facing up as you open the flap. Follow the same post office rules as for invitations.

NOTES

VII

A SPECIAL WORD TO THE GROOM

YOUR STARRING TURN

You and your parents have fewer hospitality responsibilities than the bride's family, but as a Jewish groom, you have a special role to play in the ceremony and in the surrounding festivities.

Your Torah Honor—the Oyfruf

By tradition, the bridegroom, king for a day, may be honored by a special call to read the Torah at Sabbath services (an *aliyah*) and a reception *(kiddush)* afterward. You and your parents make all the arrangements for this party, also called an *oyfruf*, which takes place on the Sabbath before the wedding.

The Torah reading will actually be done by the lay reader of the congregation. You, the groom, need only refresh your memory of the blessings before and after the reading—the same as the ones you said at your *bar mitzvah*. If you would like to do more, you can arrange to read the portion yourself, perhaps even lead the entire additional service *(musaf)*.

Your father, the bride's father, and other male members of the family (and women, in those congregations that permit women to be called up to the Torah) may also be assigned portions to read *(aliyot)*. Participation in the service is an honor. If there are family members who wish to lead part of the service, this can also be arranged in advance.

Discuss all these details with the rabbi. He will tell you how many *aliyot* you may have (there may be other celebrations in the congregation) and what amount of participation in the service he will allow. Prepare a list for the rabbi, giving the Hebrew names of all those who will be called up and give it to him during the week before the service.

Don't forget to tell those who will be honored, so they may be prepared for the reading.

The Wedding Procession

Your parents have an active part to play in the wedding ceremony by escorting you down the aisle to the *huppah*. Some young men resist this, on mistaken grounds of "dignity" or "modernity." Don't! This is one of the oldest of Jewish wedding traditions. That walk down the aisle is the actualization of your parents' dream for you, first expressed in the blessings said when you were named.

No matter what your age and place in society, if you are fortunate enough to have your parents alive to see

you married, give them this moment of totally unself-
ish joy and satisfaction (nachas). It will be your turn to
rejoice (kvell) over your own child someday. At that
happy moment, you will also understand why parents
cry at weddings.

The Wedding Vow

In Jewish wedding ceremonies, the groom recites an
ancient Aramaic wedding vow before placing the ring
on his bride's finger. In the Sephardic transliteration, it
reads:

HAREY AT MEKUDDESHET LI B'TABA'AT ZO
K'DAT MOSHE V'ISRAEL

הֲרֵי אַתְּ מְקֻדֶּשֶׁת לִי בְּטַבַּעַת זוֹ כְּדַת מֹשֶׁה וְיִשְׂרָאֵל.

Which means:

*Behold thou are consecrated unto me with this ring according to
the law of Moses and of Israel.*

Practice. You don't want to stumble over or mutter
these unfamiliar words on your wedding day.

If a double-ring ceremony is permitted in your congregation, the bride will present your ring to you at
this time with much the same vow. You may wear a
groom's ring after the wedding, even if it was not used
during the ceremony.

YOUR GUEST LIST

Go over your family's guest list with your parents, then add your own list of friends and colleagues, and get the entire list written up completely, organized and delivered *before* your fiancée's deadline. See page 47 for the "how to." Her mother will find this a new reason to treasure you, especially if you can give her a fairly accurate estimated head count even before you write the list up.

VIII

A CHAPTER
FOR THE GROOM'S
PARENTS

Mazal tov! Though you do not have the primary responsibility for the wedding hospitality itself, you have a large role to play in the wedding ceremony and in the prewedding celebrations.

Rejoice in your son's happiness. Recognize that your daughter-in-law-to-be properly has the deciding vote when there is a question about any of the arrangements. If she decides to make all the plans herself (especially if she lives in a distant city), do not feel offended or forgotten. Your splendid moment, unique to the Jewish wedding ceremony, will come as you escort your son down the aisle and stand beside him under the wedding canopy. Even the Queen of England and Prince Philip had to watch from the first pew at their son's Anglican wedding!

Especially if you also have daughters whose weddings you will be arranging someday, seize this opportunity to relax and enjoy being a highly honored guest, instead of worrying about every detail as host and hostess.

SHALL WE SHARE THE EXPENSES?

Talk this over frankly with your son. You may feel that a substantial wedding gift, the cost of fitting out the couple's new home, and perhaps paying for the wedding trip are a sufficient contribution.

On the other hand, you may want to take a larger part in the wedding hospitality (particularly if your guest list is very large) and offer a gift of the champagne, the flowers, the music, or the photos. Be careful and tactful, so that you do not seem to be making a demand for a more elaborate wedding, or to imply that the other family is ungenerous, or cannot afford the kind of wedding you expect.

The conventional division of wedding expenses and ways of sharing are discussed in Chapter IV. If your son is financially independent, you may want to help him with the expenses he assumes.

FORMAL EXCHANGE OF VISITS

Don't let shyness inhibit the proper start of your extended family relationships. The engaged pair will be married to each other and be part of each other's family for many years. The connection can be an enriching expansion of your most immediate relationships.

Start right. As soon as the couple tell you of their intentions, call her parents and arrange to visit. What do you say? Tell them how happy you are to welcome their daughter into your family. Talk about her lovable qualities. Don't be afraid to be enthusiastic. You have each loved your own children; now you also have an opportunity to cherish the person each one of them loves.

If distance separates you from the bride or her parents, write enthusiastically, welcoming your son's fiancée and extending your felicitations to her parents. Tell them how much you look forward to meeting them. If no other opportunity presents itself, you might plan to entertain both families at a prewedding dinner or a rehearsal party when you arrive for the wedding.

After the engagement is announced, you may want to give a party at which the bride will meet your family and friends. This could be a brunch or cocktail party in her honor. It is most appropriate when the engagement will be a long one, or you do not plan an *oyfruf*.

Remember that showers are not hosted by the immediate members of either family.

If you are invited to a bridal shower, bring a gift. You may receive a courtesy invitation if you live out of town. If you can, send a gift for the bride to the shower hostess.

FAMILY GIFTS

Select a personal gift to the bride from you, perhaps a piece of heirloom jewelry. You may present this to her either at the engagement party, or just before the wedding.

Decide on your wedding gift to the couple. This can be silver, furnishings for their new home, a car, a check. If a substantial sum is involved, it makes good sense to discuss it with your son, especially if you plan to help him set up a professional office, so that the couple may know what their expectations are.

Ceremonial objects are sometimes given as traditional gifts by parents and grandparents when an engagement is announced. While these are often heirlooms, they may also be purchased new. The groom may be given a *kiddush* cup or a silver spice box; the bride, a lace Sabbath scarf, or a silver cover for a prayerbook or Bible.

Just before the wedding, the groom may be presented with a man's (full size) prayer shawl *(tallit)* by the bride's parents and the bride may be given Sabbath candlesticks by his family.

WHEN YOU ARE THE WEDDING HOSTS

In some rare cases (the bride is an orphan, say, or her family lives in a remote foreign country), you may be hosting the wedding. Your invitation would be worded:

> *Mr. and Mrs. Jonathan Groom*
>
> *request the honour of your presence*
>
> *at the marriage of*
>
> *Miss Linda Bride*
>
> *to their son*
>
> *Paul Groom*

Note the use of "Miss" before the bride's name.

If her parents will be present, but you have made all the arrangements, you may decide on the traditional form, using the names of both families (see Chapter VI).

PEACEFUL PLANNING

The key word is cooperation. You may make suggestions, but accept the bride's decisions graciously. Some of the ways you can avoid friction are:

1. Stay within the number of invitations the bride's parents have allotted you. Don't strain the budget—or the space.

2. Have your guest list organized and ready on time.

3. Offer to help address the invitations, but do not feel offended if the bride decides to control the procedure by doing it herself.

4. Help in following up on those guests from your list who do not respond.

5. Give the bride your seating plan for the reception, but be flexible about it.

6. Tastes differ with generations. Respect the choices of the young couple in china, silver, and furniture for their own home. After all, they will have to live with whatever "new look" they've chosen, not you.

By the same token, their desire for a simple, possibly unconventional wedding should be seriously considered. A wedding in an arboretum, for example, can be very lovely—and very different! See Chapter XIV.

For your own happiness, don't put your son in the middle between his bride-to-be and you when a problem must be resolved. It's *his* day and your joy must stem from his.

PLANNING THE TORAH HONOR (THE OYFRUF)

Where to Hold It

Your own synagogue is the best place to hold this celebration, unless the groom does not live in the same town and prefers his own congregation.

Students can often arrange an attractive informal *oyfruf* through their college Hillel group. All synagogues and *havurah* groups will happily arrange this participation in the service. See Chapter VII for details of the observance.

Whom to Invite

It is customary to invite members of both families, friends and business associates, and in some congregations, all those present at services. Friends of other faiths may also be invited.

Invitations are informal, either by telephone, or by simple notes, and may be announced from the pulpit as well.

Arranging for Sabbath Observance

An *oyfruf* almost always takes place on the Sabbath, but you can consult with the rabbi for other possible times that are not Sabbaths. For Orthodox guests, who may not travel on this day, it is best not to make an invitation, but only a simple announcement of the fact that an *oyfruf* will take place so that they do not feel obliged to make elaborate weekend arrangements in order to attend. You may want to put up some very close relatives—grandparents or married siblings, say —for the weekend so that they can be present. The bride and her family may need the same courtesy.

Accommodations

You arrange housing for your overnight guests in a nearby hotel or motel, or with friends and neighbors. Your guests pay for their accommodations, though, as a gracious gesture, you may want to pay the bill for your closest relatives. As the hosts, you provide their weekend meals and *Shabbat* afternoon activities, since they will not be able to travel home till after dark.

There will be less tension if you do not try to cope with accommodating a houseful of overnight guests, as well as entertaining them at a *kiddush* and the Sabbath meals.

Hats and Bags

Check the synagogue practice. In Orthodox congregations, men and married women may need head coverings. Inform your guests, if they are not familiar with this procedure. Remind them also that they may not carry handbags, briefcases, umbrellas, newspapers, books, and the like in those surroundings. This is really not appropriate in any synagogue.

For a Sweet Life

Check with the sexton *(shammash)*. If the congregation permits it, you can arrange for a traditional showering of the groom with nuts and sweets when his reading is completed. A very small handful of raisins, almonds, and hard candies is placed in little white bags, securely fastened, to prevent littering the floor. They are thrown by family and close friends from the balcony or the aisle as the groom returns to his place from the pulpit and symbolize the wish for a fruitful life.

The Reception (Kiddush)

The *kiddush* can be arranged with a synagogue-approved caterer, or the sexton. If you would like to prepare the collation yourself, check carefully whether you will be permitted to bring refreshments of your own and precisely which foods will be allowed. Hospitality can range from a simple spread of nuts, fruits, sweets, cake and wine, to an elaborate buffet luncheon. Some families provide a sweet table and wine for all, so that the entire congregation may join in rejoicing with them, and then serve a luncheon for their invited guests, either in the synagogue reception rooms or at home.

Only the wine and cake are essential, so that the appropriate blessings may be said. Your decision as to the other dishes to be served will depend on how many guests you have, whether they come from a distance, and, if they are Orthodox, how you will entertain them for the rest of the day.

The blessing over the wine is usually given by the rabbi.

Checklist

1. Do you want flowers—for the synagogue, the reception table? Will the synagogue order them, or do you?

2. What table appointments do you need and who provides them? Check tablecloths, silver, serving pieces, platters, paper goods, and the like.

3. When can you bring your foods in and where will they be stored? Double-check refrigeration.

4. What help do you need for setting up and serving?

5. If you will do it yourself, what's the timetable for the day?

> Can you set up the day before?
> When will the services end?
> Is there enough time after the Torah reading to set out the refreshments? (Competent help at this point is essential, so that you can enjoy the reading and be an unflurried hostess as well.)

6. Will there be a receiving line at the conclusion of the services? (You will have to leave the preparations and come up smiling for this happy moment of congratulations.)

7. Who will clean up *(before,* as well as after)? Arrange to pay (or tip) your help either before or after the Sabbath.

8. Will leftover food be stored for you so you can take it home after the Sabbath? Provide containers beforehand.

9. Do you want to take your table flowers home after the Sabbath? Give them to a hospital or senior home? Make clear arrangements with the person in charge. Flowers for the platform *(bimah)* remain there as your gift to the synagogue.

WEDDING REHEARSAL PARTIES

When there is a planned rehearsal a day or two before the wedding, a dinner is usually given afterward by the parents of the groom for the wedding party, their husbands, wives or fiancés, and any members of the family who have come from a distance to attend the wedding.

A prewedding dinner may be given for this group when there is no rehearsal.

This is an opportunity for you to entertain and get to know "the other side," especially if you are not hosting a *kiddush*. You may have a simple buffet, an elaborate dinner with dancing, or anything in between. You will all be going to the wedding very soon after, so it is good to keep the party small, informal, relaxed, and fun for all.

Invitations are informal, but it is best to send a written note, to be sure there is no confusion as to time and place.

PLANNING FROM A DISTANCE

When you live at some distance from the town where the prewedding dinner or the *oyfruf* will take place, you will have to enlist the cooperation of the bride's family, or entrust the arrangements to your son, if he does live in the wedding area.

The bride's parents can suggest a caterer for the *kiddush*, or suitable restaurants for the rehearsal or prewedding dinner you plan to give. Deal with the caterer yourself, by phone or mail.

Checklist for a Dinner

Ask for:

several menus from which to make your selection

the wine list, or details of an open bar arrangement

complete prices for both the food and drink and the services you will require

What will the table arrangements be: T- or U-shaped or several smaller tables?

Is a private dining room or a private section available?

Is there music, or can you provide your own?

What table appointments will be provided (dishes, linens, etc.)?

Flowers and other decorations—Be specific as to your requests. Get a firm price on flowers, as prices vary considerably in different parts of the country.

Checklist for a Kiddush

Ask the bride's family or your son to check whether there is a synagogue caterer and how you may reach him. Then go over the *oyfruf* checklist with him or her.

If there is no caterer, have them find out for you:

Where can you order the food and wine you want to serve?

Where can you find paid help for the day?

Deal with these sources yourself by phone or mail.

If you will have to bring the food and disposable dishes with you, simplify! Make a list and a menu, and check and double-check before you leave home. Consider leaving a day earlier so you can do the shopping on the spot, instead of shlepping.

NOTES

IX

THE
WEDDING PARTY

THE BRIDE'S ATTENDANTS

Whom to Select

Bridesmaids should be chosen from among your relatives and close friends. Include the sisters of the groom, if you can. They'll be part of your family after the wedding.

You are under no obligation to "return the honor" and choose as attendants friends at whose wedding you have served, especially if you wish to keep the wedding party small.

The maid or matron of honor should be your sister or your closest friend.

Non-Jewish friends may serve as attendants in most congregations.

Wedding Party Gifts

It is customary to give each of the attendants (bride to bridesmaids, groom to ushers) a small personal gift as a memento of the day. The gifts should all be alike. If they are of silver or gold, they can be engraved with the date and the initials of the attendant.

Duties of the Bridesmaids

Bridesmaids, in their youthful charm, warmth, and gaiety epitomize the idea of "rejoicing with the bride." Their main duty is to be on time—for fittings, picture-taking, and the ceremony—and to be tactful and pleasant to all the guests.

Bridesmaids often plan showers for the bride.

Duties of the Maid/Matron of Honor

The maid or matron of honor has a few more duties. She will help the bride finish dressing, hold her bouquet during the ceremony, and may hold the groom's ring until it is needed, if there is to be a double-ring ceremony.

If there are both maid and matron of honor, the duties may be divided between them. If the bride's veil and train are long, they will straighten it behind her when she turns to go back down the aisle on the arm of her husband.

If there is a large bridal party, the matron of honor is responsible for checking to see that all the members have arrived, have the proper accessories and bouquets, and that they assemble promptly for picture-taking and the ceremony.

As a less emotionally involved member of the party, the matron of honor should expect to function as a cool head and a supporting presence during the inevitable last minute jitters. Tucking a "first-aid kit" of needles, thread, pins, tissues, Band-Aids (for new shoe blisters), comb and hair spray, some aspirin, and change for emergency phone calls in with her accessories is a good idea.

Flower Girls

Little girls may be dressed in any frilly party attire or in long dresses matching the bridesmaids'. Ruffled bonnets and dainty baskets for the flower petals round out a charming look.

Think twice, though, about including children in the wedding party. They should be very close relatives and old enough (at least four) to understand their function and poised enough to carry it out without tears or other embarrassment. If the reception will be in the evening, the party may run to rather late hours for youngsters. Provide a place for their mothers to retire with a cranky or sleepy child. And be prepared to share some of the glamour of your big moment with tiny scene-stealers!

THE GROOM'S ATTENDANTS

Whom to Select

Follow the same criteria as those set forth for the bride. If you can include her brothers in the party, by all means do so.

The best man should be a brother or your closest friend.

Duties of the Ushers

Seating at Jewish weddings is informal. Guests sit where they wish, except for the front row which is reserved for those in the procession who will not stand under the *huppah* and for the closest family members. The main duty of the ushers, therefore, is to serve as an honor guard during the ceremony and to assist in transportation and hospitality. If unmarried, they are expected to get the bridesmaids to the reception when it is in a different place from the ceremony and to dance with as many unescorted women guests as possible.

Ask your ushers to arrive about an hour before the ceremony for picture-taking, rehearsal (if there has been none before), and generally to assist the best man as needed.

Duties of the Best Man

The best man is responsible for the details of outfit rental: for assembling the ushers for fittings, checking to see that all have picked up the complete outfit, including all accessories, and later on, that the rented outfits have been returned.

You also help the groom dress and run any last minute errands for him. As the cool, collected member of the wedding, you hold the wedding ring till it is needed during the ceremony, check to be sure the groom has the marriage license and may carry it for him till he turns it over to the rabbi. You help in leave-taking arrangements, seeing that the luggage is ready for the car or taxi. You may even assist by driving the couple to the airport and checking to see that honeymoon reservations are in order.

At the reception, you give the first toast to the bride or the couple, usually before the cake is cut. If there are telegrams, you read those after the toast.

You are there to stave off "wedding day panic" for your best friend and cope with little emergencies by your cheerful cooperation.

The Bachelor Dinner

The bachelor dinner is arranged by the best man and the ushers, who join together to give the bride and groom a gift.

NOTES

X

WHAT
TO WEAR

THE BRIDE

The Gown

By your choice of gown, you decide the degree of formality for the rest of the wedding party. You may wear a long dress at any hour of the day and in any setting, but long veils and trains are suitable only for the most formal of weddings and the largest houses of worship.

For home and garden weddings, and in spring and summer, simple styles in sheer or lacy fabrics are most appropriate. You may opt for a street- or ballerina-length dress for a daytime wedding, if you wish.

White or ivory is always appropriate, no matter what your age or how many times you have been married before. (See Chapter XV "Second Weddings.")

Long sleeves eliminate any need for gloves. You will want to have your hands free for the ceremony.

The décolletage should be modest. A fine store will alter a style you like, if it is too décolleté, adding sleeves, lining sheer yokes, or filling in too-low necklines.

The Veil

A face veil and a head covering are required for all traditional weddings. The veil length should conform to the formality of the dress.

For a long dress, the veil may reach to the floor. For summer weddings or less formal effects, a fingertip-length veil may be worn; with street lengths, a shoulder-length veil and a very short face veil.

Floral wreaths are pretty, but be warned—they are heavy to wear and in a close, hot atmosphere, may wilt alarmingly. Silk flowers or pearl ornaments are often used instead. A crown or tiaralike headdress is a favorite because of the tradition that both bride and groom wore golden crowns on their wedding day.

Rented Gowns

In some areas, bridal outfits may be rented. Besides the obvious economy, this echoes an ancient Jewish tradition by which betrothed girls wore borrowed finery at the celebration of engagements announced just after Yom Kippur.

If you rent your gown and veil, be careful to select an outfit that is not too opulent for the scale of your ceremony and reception. Leave the long trains for royal weddings!

Handbags

You will not carry your handbag during the ceremony, but you will want one, possibly two. Choose a small, dressy white bag to hold your "necessaries." Leave it in the bridal room until after the ceremony.

Some bridal dressmakers will provide a matching drawstring bag for the safekeeping of the many money-gift envelopes you will be handed during the reception. If you don't want to carry such a bag, pass all your gifts along to your husband or your father to hold in an inside jacket pocket.

Shoes

Choose shoes you can stand in comfortably and break them in before the wedding.

The Finishing Touches

Go easy on your makeup. This is not the day for a startling "new look" or an experimental hairdo. You will be adorned with flowers and veiling—best to keep everything simple, including your jewelry. Your loveliest ornament will be your smiling radiance on this happy day. This special inner glow is the secret ingredient that makes every bride beautiful.

THE MOTHERS

Since both mothers will walk down the aisle and stand under the *huppah*, their dresses should be the same length and of harmonizing colors. For a day wedding, they usually wear street length dresses, even if the bride wears a long gown.

For late afternoon weddings (after 4 P.M.), you may choose a cocktail dress or a long dinner gown, since the reception will go on into the evening hours.

Full formal wear is only suitable for an evening wedding at which the bride wears a formal gown.

For garden and home weddings, less formal, dressy outfits are indicated. You may want to carry out a rustic theme if that is the bride's choice.

The bride's mother decides on the length and color she prefers and informs the mother of the groom. If you have become really friendly and live in the same city, you may even shop together to simplify coordination, but it is not de rigueur. Some women may remain better friends if they do *not* shop together!

Head coverings are required in traditional settings. A small dressy hat, a twist of matching tulle and silk flowers or feathers, or a matching pillbox are all appropriate. You may remove the hat at the reception if you wish.

Gloves are optional.

A small dressy handbag may be used, but it is not carried during the ceremony.

You will be standing for hours. Select your shoes with comfort as well as style in mind and break them in before the big day. Dyeing sometimes makes shoes feel a bit stiff and tight until they have been worn for a while.

THE BRIDE'S ATTENDANTS

You, as the bride, select the color and style of the attendants' dresses, though you may want to take one or two of them with you for the preliminary shopping. Choose a simple style and a color combination that will be flattering to all.

It is not necessary to dress all the bridesmaids exactly alike. You can settle on a complementary color scheme and a few harmonizing styles and let the bridesmaids choose from among them the dress each one thinks will be most flattering to her.

Décolletage should be modest. A matching little cape or jacket is often worn during the ceremony over a low-cut formal gown.

The maid or matron of honor's dress is usually in a contrasting color and a slightly more elaborate style.

A junior bridesmaid or flower girl should wear a harmonizing dress in a style suited to her age. Avoid the look of a cut-down adult evening gown.

Though they need not wear head coverings, it makes for a more finished look if your attendants are all turned out alike. Select a simple headpiece with this in mind. Also decide on the pumps or sandals that are to be dyed to match the dress and select an appropriate shade of hose. Gloves are optional.

When you have made your decision, arrange to have all the attendants meet at the bridal shop at one time for a fitting. The hemlines should be coordinated by the fitter. This is easier if the actual shoes or heels of the same height are worn for the fitting.

A good bridal shop will provide the services of a consultant who will coordinate all the details of matching accessories and keep track of the fitting schedule.

Bridesmaids and the matron or maid of honor pay for their own outfits. If the dresses are a style that can be worn again after the wedding, they will be even happier to serve as members of the wedding party.

If there is a friend you particularly want as a bridesmaid and you feel she may not be able to afford her outfit, you may offer (tactfully!) to make it a gift to her.

You may decide with the bridesmaids that they will make their own outfits. Select a simple style; be sure everyone uses the same pattern and that they purchase the fabrics together, to be certain the dresses are coordinated. Simple ballerina-length full skirts and frilly blouses (which can be purchased) make for a very pretty informal look.

A Panic-Stopper List

To avoid confusion and misunderstandings, type out a list of instructions for each attendant.

1. Name and telephone number of store and salesperson's name

2. Pick up your dress _____ (date)

3. Pick up your shoes _____ (date)

4. Please break in your new shoes!

5. Party schedule (if they will be expected to attend)

6. Time and place of rehearsal (if there is one)

7. Time and place of rehearsal party

8. Time and place where bridesmaids will finish dressing for the ceremony

9. Transportation arrangements from wedding to reception (if required)

Also, make a list for yourself with each attendant's phone number.

THE GROOM

The groom's outfit is determined by the formality of the bride's choice.

Less Formal Weddings

A dark business suit with a fine white shirt and elegant tie is suitable for all but the most formal weddings.

Dinner jackets (tuxedos) are not worn before 6 P.M., but an exception may be made at weddings that begin at 4 P.M. and go on into the evening hours.

Formal Attire

When the bride wears a long formal gown and veil, the groom wears:

for day weddings:	morning suit, or Oxford gray jacket and striped trousers, or gray cutaway and trousers
for evening weddings:	black tie—dinner jacket, or white tie—tails
for summer weddings:	blazer and white flannels, or white dinner jacket, black formal trousers

Accessories and hats to match.

The dress of the other men in the party is determined by the groom's choice.

Avant-Garde Dress

Avant-garde formal wear is now readily available from rental outfitters. One in Manhattan advertises sixty different styles! Make a thoughtful choice that will flatter all the men, bearing in mind that both fathers should wear the same style. Consider carefully whether your company of ushers, best man, and the fathers, all togged out in brightly colored outfits and ruffled shirts, may not look like a TV singing group.

Informal dress of a relaxed, colorful nature may be flowered shirts, matching vests, and trousers, or variations on peasant outfits. Such choices should be carefully coordinated with the bride's in color, fabric, and overall look. If you select a very youthful, avant-garde style, will your father and hers look right in it? Can they appropriately wear conventional formal or semi-formal wear or dark business suits instead?

All-White

Yes, a groom may dress in an all-white outfit, as befits Jewish solemnity. The other men of the party may dress in white, or in suitable summer wear if it is a summer wedding, or in business suits or formal wear appropriate for other seasons of the year.

MEN OF THE WEDDING PARTY

Formal outfits, for yourself as well as your attendants are often rented. Make the arrangements about a month in advance, so the necessary fittings and alterations can be done. Meet the ushers, best man, and the two fathers at the outfitter's and have all fitted at the same time.

Hats are an essential part of the man's outfit. They should all be the same. Decide whether you are going to wear top hats (formal), Homburgs or fedoras (business suits), panamas (summer wear) or fancy skullcaps *(yarmulkes).* With the newest colorful informal attire, the velvet or satin skullcap is probably the best choice.

Black (or white for summer) dress shoes should be the choice for all. If they are new, be sure they are broken in before the wedding. You will all be standing for a long time.

Ties or ascots for the ushers should be alike; the best man's and the groom's may be different.

Gloves are optional.

Junior attendants may wear their best dark suits, or if they are very young, any colorful outfit that is appropriate.

A good rental agency will provide complete coordination and all the accessories you need. Fittings should be meticulous, especially since the back of the suit will be seen for a long time during the service, and a poorly fitting jacket becomes very noticeable.

Checklist for Rented Outfits

Does the jacket neck fit without gapping?

Does the jacket back hang without wrinkles or bulges?

Are the sleeves the right length, reaching to the same place on each man's arm?

Are the trouser lengths coordinated?

If hats are to be rented, does each man have the correct size?

What choice is there in ascots and ties?

Does each man know how to tie the one chosen?

Will you rent shirts or use your own best whites?

Who supplies separate collars (for formal neckband-type shirts)?

Do you need studs and cuff links?

Ushers and the best man pay for their own outfits.

The Groom's Panic-Stopper List

Make an instruction sheet for each usher.

1. Name, address, phone number of the rental agency, fitter's name

2. Pick up your outfit on _____ (date)

3. Please break in new shoes!

4. Party schedule (if they are expected to attend)

5. Time and place of the rehearsal (if there will be one)

6. Time and place of the rehearsal party

7. Assemble at _____ (place) _____ (time) for the ceremony

8. Transportation arrangements from ceremony to reception (if necessary)

9. The boutonniere goes on the left lapel. Pin it on.

10. *Don't forget your hat!*

Also make a list for yourself with the name and phone number of each attendant.

NOTES

PERSONAL BUSINESS

FOR THE BRIDE

Your New Name

Brides today have a number of options in the name they use after marriage. Many are quite happy to follow convention and take their husband's name. Others, seeking not to erase the persona they have developed over years of schooling and the start of a career, decide to keep their own names in the business world, and sometimes socially as well. This is legal in most states.

Another alternative is the hyphenated name. Beverly Feld would thus become Beverly Feld-Brown after her marriage to Paul Brown, who may also opt to use the hyphenated name as an egalitarian measure. Children are usually given the hyphenated name.

If you decide to change your name, you must arrange to have it changed on all your legal records, credit cards, and identification. A few weeks before the wedding, arrange to have your name changed by:

1. the Social Security Administration

2. the Motor Vehicle bureau, if you drive. If you own your own car, have the registration changed as well as your driver's license.

3. issuers of credit cards and charge accounts

4. your bank. You will need new checks if you change the name on your account.

5. your employer

Some of these may ask to see your marriage certificate as evidence for the name change. In that case, take care of the change as soon after the wedding as possible.

How do you sign your name? If you are keeping your own name, no change is necessary. You remain Beverly Feld. If you are using your husband's name socially, you style yourself Mrs. Paul Brown for those occasions.

Otherwise, you sign your name Beverly F. Brown (or Beverly Feld-Brown for the hyphenated name) on all checks and legal papers. To friends who know your new name, you may sign yourself Beverly Brown.

If you have not had credit cards before marriage, be sure to open joint charge accounts in both your husband's name and yours—Beverly F. Brown, *not* Mrs. Paul Brown. If you are changing the name on your own accounts, follow the same rule. This is the only way a married woman can assure herself of developing her own credit record, most important in case of divorce or a spouse's death. If you are employed, there is no reason why you cannot have a charge account in your name only.

Stationery

You will need a new stationery outfit in any case, showing your new address and your chosen name. Include:

1. business letter paper for everyday use

2. informals with your monogram or name. You can use your name alone, Mr. and Mrs., or both your names on one line as

Beverly Feld and Paul Brown

3. fine quality letter paper, plain or with your monogram

Monograms

For linens and stationery, use the initial letters of your first name, your maiden surname, and your husband's surname—the last being the largest or center letter of the monogram.

For silver, use only the initial letter of your new surname or the three-letter style above.

Only for informal use do you combine your husband's and your first name initials (as on paper party ware or bar glasses).

If you are keeping your own name or hyphenating

it, you might experiment with a four-letter monogram, in which the two center initials, larger, are those of your two surnames, with the appropriate first name initials on either side.

FOR BOTH BRIDE AND GROOM

(Before the Wedding)

More important, in many ways than your gown, your reception, and the like, are the practical details involved in the new household you are forming. Somewhere in the flurry of events before your wedding you will, if you are wise, make time to attend to all the matters listed below. Make appointments, enter them in your calendar, and *keep* them. As with the wedding procession itself, when you start your new life together, start off on the right foot!

1. Draw up your wills. Every person (male *or* female) should have a will, if only to leave everything to the spouse and appoint an executor to serve without fee.

2. Discuss life insurance for each. If you already have insurance, change the beneficiaries. Is the amount enough for the responsibilities of a married person?

3. Arrange joint bank accounts and a safe deposit box with entry rights for both of you.

4. Have dental and physical checkups. Arrange for blood tests in time to conform with local rules.

5. Decide on your new home and arrange to have utilities and phone ready for the move in.

6. Arrange for insurance on the house or apartment and your gifts.

7. Find your birth certificate. Keep it together with your blood test papers, ready to take with you when you go to get your marriage license.

Be patient and of good cheer! When the fussy details have been attended to, you will enjoy a beautiful wedding and a happy "ever after."

NOTES

XII

WEDDING GIFTS

Generous wedding gifts, usually of money, are in the Jewish tradition. Plan with your fiancé to open a joint account for the deposit of your checks and cash. Also arrange for the safekeeping of any bonds you receive. Do this well before the wedding, as gifts will start to come in to the bride's home before the big day.

RECORD-KEEPING

Keep a record of each gift received in your bride's book. If there is time, start writing your thank-you notes for every gift that arrives before the wedding. Check them off, as you finish them. You will have many more to write after the wedding.

GIFT LISTS

To be sure of receiving the gifts you really want, you and your fiancé should make up a list and give it to the bride's mother or sister. Include on it your china and silver patterns and color schemes. The list keeper should not hesitate to offer suggestions to a guest who inquires. If the guest didn't want to be sure of giving a much-desired present, he or she wouldn't have asked!

Note on the list who is expected to be giving the gift you suggested, to avoid duplications. No one wants six food processors!

If you would truly prefer a money gift, the family may very properly suggest this alternative, if asked. It is tactful to mention that the couple do not know yet where they will live, or are moving to a distant area, or that they hope to use their cash gifts toward a major household purchase.

Some department stores and specialty shops maintain a bridal registry where a bride may indicate her preferences in china and silver patterns, and color schemes for table, bath, and bed linens. While your mother or sister may tell friends of the listing, you should never allow the shop to send out a mailing announcing that you have registered with them.

EXCHANGING GIFTS

Gifts may be exchanged, but this is touchy. Asking the giver to exchange a present he or she has gone to some trouble to select may result in hurt feelings, not to mention inconvenience.

If you can discreetly exchange the gift yourself, it is correct to do so, especially if you have been given duplicate items. Unless you are asked specifically later, you need not tell people you have made an exchange. You write your thank-you note for the original gift.

THANK-YOU NOTES

Every gift you receive must be acknowledged with a thank-you note, even if you have thanked the giver personally at the reception. Can you really remember all the people you spoke with at the reception? Will they remember your verbal thanks?

All your notes should be written as promptly as possible, within one month after the wedding.

Not to acknowledge gifts, or to be very tardy in doing so, is extremely rude and can cause serious rifts with friends and relatives. When your guests have gone to trouble and expense to salute your marriage, the very least you can do is put forth the effort it takes to respond promptly.

Don't think of it as one hundred letters all at once—regard it as five a day for twenty days! With weekends off, that makes a month in which to respond. A thank-you note need contain only three sentences. And there's no reason why your husband cannot share this task. The gifts were for him, too. If he's shy at writing, let him stamp, seal, check off, and mail the letters for you. Working together makes the task go lightly.

A Model Note

Write your notes on white, ivory, or gray informal folders in blue or black ink. If you use livelier color combinations, be sure your pen matches the border or the monogram. Never, never type.

The three necessary sentences (and a fourth optional) after the salutation are:

1. *Thank you for your beautiful (cut glass bowl,* etc.) or *your generous check, bond,* etc. (do not mention the dollar amount)

2. *It will be just right for our new living room* (or some other sentence that indicates how you will use the gift)

or, for a money gift

We are planning to use it toward our new stereo system (or whatever large purchase you have in mind).

3. *Marvin and I appreciate your thoughtfulness.*

4. (Optional) *We hope you will visit us soon. You will see your gift* (or, name the object) *in a place of honor in our new home.*

Close the note *Cordially,* or *Affectionately,* (for family).

You may vary the sentences as you please, as long as you cover these main points.

If your husband writes some of the notes, he mentions your name in sentence three. Whoever writes the note signs it, first name only for close friends and relatives, full name for others.

USING CARDS

You may use a printed thank-you card, but it is most thoughtful and courteous to add a personal sentence, such as "The cut glass bowl is lovely!" before you sign the card with both your names.

INSURANCE FOR GIFTS

If you receive many gifts, consider taking out a floater insurance policy to cover them wherever they are stored and also while they are in your car.

You may also want to have someone stand guard over the house or apartment where you have stored them during the actual wedding period. When a wedding receives a great deal of publicity, thieves find the wedding day the ideal time to steal property from a house that is empty during the festivities. A new home that is unoccupied during the honeymoon is another favorite spot for burglaries. (See Chapter XIII "Newspaper Announcements.")

NOTES

XIII

NEWSPAPER ANNOUNCEMENTS

Local newspapers, Jewish papers (English and Yiddish), and local weeklies may be used to publish the announcement of a wedding (or of an engagement). Be sure to allow enough time in advance, at least a week, and more for publication out of town or overseas.

FORMS AND RELEASES

Many newspapers have standard announcement forms for you to fill out. Call the society editor for a copy about two weeks beforehand and carefully check deadline dates. Will they use the bride's picture? What are the photo regulations? Can you order extra copies of the paper on the day?

Never give information over the phone without formalizing it in writing. Errors in print are embarrassingly permanent.

If there is no form, send in a complete press release. Copy the format of the society pages of that particular paper. Be sure to identify your release by putting the name, address, and phone number of the person responsible for the story in the upper right corner of the page. Newspapers in large cities often phone to verify the release.

PHOTOS

Identify your photo with a taped-on cover sheet giving the name of the bride, married to _____ on _____. And for additional insurance, lightly write the name in pencil on the back of the photo itself, together with the photo credit. The picture will, in most cases, not be returned, whether it is used or not.

If you do not want to be photographed in your wedding gown before the wedding day, you may use an engagement photo or any other picture of yourself that you like.

SOME SPECIAL PROBLEMS

Shall you mention:

A Previous Marriage?
Yes. As:
    "Ms. Taylor's previous marriage ended in divorce."
or

"Mrs. Berlin is the widow of the late Charles Alter of Denver."

Children of a Previous Marriage?
As you choose. As:

"He has two children by the marriage, Alice and Jeffrey."

or

"She has one child by the marriage, Gabriel Alter."

Deceased Parents?
Yes. As:

"Miss Sarah Brown, daughter of Mr. (or Mrs.) Martin Brown and the late Mrs. (or Mr.) Brown."

or, when the mother has remarried

". . . married to Mr. Paul Silver, son of Mrs. Joseph Marcus of Chicago and the late Walter Silver of Denver."

Both Parents When They Are Divorced?
Yes. As:

"Mr. Robert Lavin, son of Mrs. Mildred Lavin of New York and Mr. Arthur Lavin of Baltimore."

or, when the mother has remarried

"Miss Miriam Bloom, daughter of Mrs. Peter Abel of Albany and Mr. Harry Bloom of Buffalo."

When the remarried couple are named as announcing the wedding:

"Mr. and Mrs. Peter Abel announce the marriage of her daughter, Miriam Bloom, to . . . The bride is the daughter also of Mr. Harry Bloom of Buffalo."

A Legally Changed Name?

As you choose. As:

"Mr. Richard Meadows, son of Mr. and Mrs. Bernard Medovsky. Mr. Meadows changed his name legally."

However, this last sentence is not necessary, since a person has the right to change his name. The difference between the names of the parents and the son makes the legality of the name change obvious.

The Bride Keeping Her Own Name?

Yes. As:

"The bride will retain her own name professionally."

A Hyphenated Name?

Yes. As:

"The couple will use the name Bloom-Lavin."

The Address of Your New Home?

No. **Especially not** if you mention plans for a wedding trip. This is an open invitation to thieves, advertising a newly furnished, unoccupied home.

Exception: If you will be moving out of town, the location may be given, but **not** the street address.

As:

"Mr. and Mrs. Lavin will live in Denver."

XIV

UNCONVENTIONAL WEDDINGS

CHANGING THE RITUAL

Many arguments can be heard for "equalizing" or modernizing the wedding service. Though it may be fashionable to write "nonchauvinist" vows or contracts, or to interpolate exotic readings or odd bits of ritual from other faiths, you should think carefully before you follow the fad.

Very rarely will a rabbi allow any changes in the ritual or the legal formula of the Jewish ceremony. They were developed over the centuries to make clear the rights and obligations of both parties to a contract, to provide maximum legal protection for both husband and wife, and to sanctify this legal relationship with blessings, making it a holy bond, an exchange of vows that is dignified, impressive, and poetic.

Some rabbis will permit the interpolation of personal readings after the ring ceremony, or as an addition to the Seven Wedding Blessings.

Do the writings of Kahlil Gibran rank with King Solomon's Song of Songs? Choose what is meaningful to you and most appropriate to this deeply significant moment. Think of the countless thousands of Jewish men and women who, for centuries, have joined their lives together under the *huppah* with the same vows. You may decide that the truest emotional meaning derives from forging one more link in the unbroken chain of Jewish experience that reaches back to Isaac and Rebekah.

UNUSUAL SETTINGS

You may seek to set up your wedding canopy under the open sky in unusual locations, from your garden to a grassy meadow or the deck of a chartered yacht. One couple recently tried to hold their ceremony at the bus stop where they first met!

If you depart from conventional festivities, you must carefully plan every step so that your special day will be as near perfect as you can make it.

Study the description of the traditional ceremony (Chapter II). Be sure that your plans will accommodate the essential elements of a Jewish wedding. Check out the reminders below.

Choosing the Site

1. Is the place reasonably accessible?

2. Is there sufficient off-the-road parking?

3. What cover is there in case of rain or inclement weather? Is there shade for an excessively hot day?

4. Is there adequate privacy from wandering hikers, picnickers, or uninvited onlookers?

5. If you select a public park, do you need a permit? How far in advance?

6. Can you hold your reception in the same place? If not, can you arrange a car pool to transport your guests from one central meeting place to the ceremony and then to the reception?

Choosing the Officiant

1. How much extra time will this excursion demand of him or her?

2. Will the officiant be agreeable to the demands of the site (climbing a hill, sailing on a yacht)?

3. What ritual accessories will you have to provide (huppah, wine and goblets, table and cloth, glass to break)?

4. Discuss your plans (including the refreshments) with your rabbi, to be sure he approves of your planned ceremony. If the food is not kosher, some rabbis will not perform the ceremony; others will not officiate outside their synagogues.

5. Since sound carries poorly out of doors, make some arrangements to be sure the service will be heard.

THE INVITATIONS

You may select any colorful, informal invitation that pleases you and carries out the theme or design your own.

Be sure you include:

1. Travel directions and a map. If it is a little known or out-of-the-way place, add travel time from some well-known point so guests can plan accurately for a timely arrival.

2. The alternate location in case of rain. Whom can guests call on the day, to check, if the weather is uncertain?

3. Car pool arrangements, if you plan one.

4. Address and time of reception, if it will be in a different location from the ceremony.

5. R.S.V.P. and information phone number.

REFRESHMENTS

1. If the location does not lend itself to serving a reception collation, plan to open a few bottles of champagne or wine to toast the couple (you'll need disposable glasses) and have the other food and drink served elsewhere.

Note: If you are using a public park, botanical garden,

or greenhouse, you may not be allowed to serve alcoholic beverages—or any refreshments at all. Check.

2. Arrange for coolers for wine and portable refrigeration for any food you will be serving. If you are using a caterer, specify refrigeration. If you are doing it yourself, you can use picnic coolers.

3. Concentrate on elegant picnic fare, finger foods, and little sandwiches. Avoid custards, cream sauces, and whipped cream, and have a sugar frosting on your cake to avoid worries about spoiling.

4. Plan for a picnic atmosphere. Remember there may be no kitchen nearby. You will need at least one table to spread your feast.

5. Can you pack everything well in advance? Make a list and double-check. You will need:

folding tables and chairs (if you have the transport)
plastic sheets or cushions for seating
plastic glasses, cutlery, dishes, and paper goods
serving pieces, especially a knife for the cake
garbage bags for the cleanup
containers for leftovers

6. If you are counting on friends and family for help, delegate specific functions for the day. One person should be in charge of the serving team, another *responsible* person should head the cleanup crew.

MUSIC

Portable music is important to create the mood—serious, festive, or rustic.

Tapes and tape playback equipment will give you a wide choice of recorded selections. Check the availability of electricity or use fresh batteries.

Stringed instruments, guitars, flute, or accordion are easily transported instruments. You might want a string trio.

If friends offer their talents, accept happily. Include photos of their performances as part of your thank-you note.

PHOTOS

Arrange for photos. If you cannot find a professional photographer who will make the trip, provide film for as many photographer friends as you can muster. Some of the pictures, if not all, will be superb records of this unique day. Your principal photographer will earn a thank-you note and gift copies of the best shots in appreciation of his skill.

XV

SECOND WEDDINGS

Jewish thought regards the newly single state of the widowed or divorced as undesirable. Second or subsequent weddings are therefore approached with the same feelings of joy as the first. The celebration may be a bit more restrained if the couple are older, or if one of the pair has only recently been widowed, but the same degree of honor is paid to them.

THE CEREMONY

The ceremony is the same as for a first wedding. Parents, if they are still alive, escort the bride or groom to the *huppah*. If there are no parents surviving, a close friend or relative may escort either one and also serve as best man or matron of honor.

A young bride may have as many bridesmaids as she wishes (especially if she is marrying again after a hasty first marriage and divorce), but a more mature bride usually dispenses with attendants except for the escort.

If the ceremony will be a very simple one at home or in the rabbi's study and there are no parents, the bride and groom may simply take their places before the officiant for the service in the presence of their family and friends. Since there is no recessional, they turn and face the company to receive their congratulations and lead the way to the reception they are hosting.

DRESS

No matter what her age is, or how many times she has been married before, a Jewish bride may always correctly wear white. The color is a symbol of the solemnity of the day, not of virginity. Similarly, a second bride wears a veil and head covering (required in traditional practice, optional in others). A more mature woman wisely chooses off-white or ivory shades, a simple cap and shorter veil, and a more sophisticated gown. A becoming hat is also appropriate where a veil is not required. No matter how slender the bride may be, it is probably best to leave the ruffled and flounced dresses to the very young.

The groom and the other members of the bridal party follow the guidelines set down in Chapter X.

PAYING FOR THE SECOND WEDDING

A mature bride and groom may decide to share the costs, or the groom, as host, may pay them all. Parents of the bride do not usually pay for a second wedding unless the bride is a very young woman or the couple cannot assume all of the cost themselves.

Flowers, music, food, and drink may be as elaborate as you wish. A joyful reception is in the best tradition.

CHILDREN AT SECOND WEDDINGS

Should your children be present when you marry again? Yes, no, or maybe!

In some Sephardic communities, the children of a remarrying couple are excluded from the wedding. But in most communities, the children are happily present as guests, or even as attendants, if they are old enough.

The "maybe" aspect is that your decision should depend on sensitively perceived feelings. When there has been a divorce, an older child may feel a strain on his or her loyalty to the ex-spouse, who still remains the child's parent. The spouse who has custody sometimes objects to the child's attending the wedding. When a parent has died, the child may experience a renewal of grief at this time and not be ready for the rejoicing and the prospect of having a stepparent.

Be guided by how your own child feels. A reluctant

or ambivalent adolescent should, for example, not be coerced into being an attendant. A little girl or boy may be capable of serving as a flower girl or ring boy, but a caring relative should be asked to stand by as a resource, should emotional or behavior problems surface as the festivities proceed. Even an older child may be glad of the solicitous arm of a loving aunt or uncle when feelings well up. There is always some sorrow and loss underlying the joy of a second marriage.

If you can, by all means include your children in your plans. It will assure them that your new marriage does not mean yet another loss to them.

Rejoice in your new life!

XVI

THE RECEPTION

THE RECEIVING LINE

The receiving line is slowly falling into disuse except at the most formal of large weddings in liberal congregations, or when there will be a cocktail and buffet reception for most of the guests, and a private family dinner later. Since no food should be served until all have passed along the receiving line, the time can become tedious for guests. It is also most fatiguing for members of the wedding party.

When there is a receiving line, it is arranged this way:

> Bride's mother (first)
> Groom's father (optional)
> Groom's mother
> Bride's father (optional)
> Bride

> Groom
> Maid/Matron of Honor
> Bridesmaids

Ushers and the best man do not join the line. Fathers often choose not to stand in the line but to circulate among the guests to greet them, see that champagne or some other drinks are available, and, together with the ushers, see that guests who are alone are introduced to others.

What to Say

Your guests will congratulate you. Thank them cordially and add some phrases indicating how happy you are that they could come to the wedding. Then turn and introduce your guest to the next person on the receiving line. This is not the time for lingering personal conversations.

You and your mother should take care to present members of your family and your friends to your new husband and his mother, and vice versa. If you do not know a guest's name, ask graciously. No one should be passed along as a nameless Mr. or Ms.—Ummmm.

Expect to be kissed. Some enthusiastic aunts may even kiss the groom!

When There Is No Receiving Line

The bride and groom often observe a brief seclusion after the ceremony (whether for the traditional *Yihud* or for picture-taking) and there is no receiving line. Instead there is a short cocktail hour during which the parents greet the guests. After everyone has been seated in the dining room (or after a brief interval at a buffet reception), the bride and groom enter to a fanfare from the musicians. As soon as they are seated, the meal service may begin.

SEATING ARRANGEMENTS

The Bride's Table

Even if the reception will be a tea or cocktail buffet, you may want to have a bride's table for your wedding party so that you may be served a seated meal.

Your parents may have a separate table, if they wish, with the groom's parents as guests of honor and including the grandparents, the rabbi and his wife, and any other honored guests. The size of the wedding party is usually the deciding factor.

Other Tables

Though you will want to seat family members together, it is important to look out for the occasional friend who does not know the family, or out-of-town relatives who may not know many people, and arrange to seat them with a congenial group. In a large family, the principal family members may be seated at different tables where they act as assistant hosts and see to it that all are introduced around.

Divorced Parents

(See Chapter XVII.)

THE REPAST

Blessing over Bread

It is traditional to begin the meal with the blessing *(hamotzi)* said over the large braided wedding loaf (the *hallah)*. The *hallah* is set on the bridal table or the center of the buffet. You may want to honor a grandfather or uncle with the ceremonial recitation of the blessing and cutting of the *hallah.* Some couples do this as their first act of hospitality as bride and groom. The loaf is cut and slices distributed to all the tables so that all may share it.

Dancing

When dance music is provided, there is a formal first dance (usually a waltz) in which the bride and groom dance together for the first time as man and wife. They are then joined by their parents and finally the attendants. The groom always dances with both mothers, the bride with both fathers, taking turns around the dance floor.

You may want to have the traditional circle and *mitz-vah* dances and where appropriate, the *mazinkeh-tants.* (See Chapter II.) Give the leader of the musicians a list of the dances and traditional tunes you want.

Toasts

The best man offers the first toast to the couple when the champagne has been poured for all. He may also call on grandfathers and others to offer toasts and introduce other members of the wedding party, who may wish to congratulate the couple. At a small wedding, he may name a toast-maker for each table and ask him or her to say a few words of greeting—a good wish, a welcome to the new member of the family, or a happy anecdote all serve well. People who will be called upon should be given some notice, so that their brief remarks are not totally unprepared.

The best man and the groom should go over the list of toasts together and write out the names in order on a card, to avoid embarrassing lapses of memory.

Cutting the Cake

The wedding cake is cut when the dessert is served. The bride makes the first cut, assisted by the groom, with a ribbon-and-flower-decorated cake knife. They share the first slice, with the bride usually feeding the groom a bite or two. The cake is then taken off to the kitchen to be cut and served by the catering staff. At a home wedding, you may have a friend or the person in charge of serving cut the rest of the cake.

The top layer may be a fruit or spice cake which is taken off, set aside, and wrapped for the freezer, so that you may enjoy it on your first wedding anniversary.

What will you do with the leftover cake? It is no

longer boxed and given to guests. Putting it up in paper napkins is sloppy in the extreme. It is best to arrange to have it taken home, where your parents can serve it during *sheva brokhes* (if you will be observing this custom—discussed later) or it can be put in the freezer to use for your own first hospitality in your new home.

During the time the cake is being served, bride and groom make the rounds of the tables, greeting all their guests and introducing each other (especially important if there has been no receiving line). Parents usually circulate in this way as well.

Leave-taking

Unless the wedding reception has run on to a very late hour, no one should leave until the cake has been cut, and, at traditional weddings, until the Grace after meals has been said.

The bride and groom do not leave until the Grace has been completed and most of their guests have left.

If the wedding is being held in the evening at a hotel, you may want to reserve a room there and start your wedding trip the next day. Often this is part of the "package" offered by a hotel caterer.

Grace (Sheva Brokhes)

Seven days of feasting after a wedding have been a tradition among the observant since biblical times. At each meal, during these days, the seven wedding blessings (Hebrew—*sheva berakhot)* are added to the grace after meals, so the feasting came to be called, in colloquial Yiddish, *sheva brokhes.*

The first recitation of these blessings at the wedding feast is marked by a special ritual. It is an honor to be asked to lead the Grace or to recite one of the Seven Blessings. At modern traditional weddings, this ritual is followed only at the first wedding meal, the reception. Decide in advance who is to be honored and give a list to the person who will lead the Grace.

Special Grace booklets, *(bentshers)* some lavishly illustrated, containing the text in Hebrew and English can be ordered, imprinted with the names of the bride and groom and the date of the wedding. They are given to the guests as keepsakes.

Watch the Clock!

If you will be paying for music or service by the hour, be sure to have the caterer or a close relative remind you when the overtime is about to begin. Decide then whether you want to continue service or music.

NOTES

XVII

WHEN PARENTS ARE DIVORCED

Unless they have not spoken for years, an ex-spouse should be invited to the wedding. He or she is still the parent of the child to be married.

For this one day, a divorced couple should resolve to bury their differences for the sake of their child. Each one is entitled to participate in and rejoice in the happiness of the child's wedding, even if the parents are no longer married to each other.

If there has been a second marriage, the new spouse attends as a guest. (So, too, with live-togethers.)

Some awkward situations will present themselves, but they can all be resolved in the true Jewish spirit of rejoicing.

SHARING THE COST

A divorced father who has remained on good terms with his ex-wife may offer to pay some or all of the costs of the wedding of his daughter. This is optional, depending on the extent of the past support he has provided and the wedding gift he intends to give.

THE PROCESSION

A divorced mother and father, forgetting their grievances, should escort their son or daughter to the *huppah*. If either is remarried, the new spouse is seated with the other guests during the ceremony.

In hostile situations, where the ex-spouse is not invited to the wedding, the mother or father may escort the bride or groom without a partner, especially if not remarried. If you have lived with a parent's second spouse for many years and feel that he or she is like a mother or father, you may ask him or her to participate and be an escort if the ex-husband or wife will not be present.

Only the grandparents in the original family are usually honored in the procession. Parents of a second spouse are not blood relatives. However, your own feelings about them should be the deciding factor.

In complicated situations, where an ex-spouse or several sets of grandparents may be present, it is sometimes best to dispense with honors to grandpar-

ents. This may avoid hurt feelings at some being excluded, while others are honored.

THE RECEIVING LINE

If there is a receiving line, a divorced father may opt
not to stand in the line, since it is optional for fathers.
If he is sharing the cost, he may function as a host
among those waiting to pass through the line.

TABLE ARRANGEMENTS

When there has been a divorce, it may be less awkward to dispense with the family table. The bride and
groom may have a table with the bridesmaids and
ushers, and if it is a small group, their spouses or fiancés.

The parents and grandparents may each host a different table of relatives and friends. An ex-husband or
wife would then be seated (with his or her new
spouse, if remarried) at a separate table of friends or
relatives from that side of the family.

NOTES

XVIII

THE BUSINESS SIDE OF YOUR WEDDING

THE CATERER

Your budget, the size, and style of your wedding will shape your decision about catering. For a small home wedding, you may need only some extra help, rented furnishings, and some or all of the food prepared by party cooks for you. You may have everything catered in for an elaborate party at home. For a large formal wedding, you will need the full services of the best caterer your budget permits.

Meeting Requirements of Kashrut

Your choices will also be defined by the customs and requirements of the Jewish community and those of observant family members. Traditional practice mandates kosher food and wines, and such synagogues often will allow you to use only the caterers they approve as properly observing the dietary laws.

Other congregations may allow a choice of caterers, but restrict the menu to dishes that are not in themselves forbidden *(tref)*; that is, they will not allow you to serve pork or shellfish, and sometimes forbid all meats as well.

Hotels and clubs usually have their own banquet services, both kosher and nonkosher. Restaurants vary. Usually, if there is no kosher meal service available, you can arrange for a vegetarian, dairy, or fish meal. Be sure you specify: no shellfish or swordfish, no meat stocks (as in aspics), or garnishes (as bacon bits), no meat or seafood in fillings for crepes, egg rolls, quiches, curries, and the like. Traditional Orthodox practice does not accept such a meal as kosher because the dishes may have been used for nonkosher foods at other times.

Choosing a theme, as a Mediterranean, Indian, or Chinese feast, can make these nonmeat meals original and festive.

Supervision

When an establishment outside a synagogue represents itself as kosher, ask what supervision is being given.

Is the kitchen under the supervision of a recognized rabbinical authority?

Is a *kashrut* supervisor *(mashgiach)* present during the food preparation and service?

Part of the higher cost of kosher food derives from

this necessary supervision. Be sure you are getting it, if you are paying for it.

"Kosher-style" refers only to the way in which foods are cooked, not to supervision. "Kosher-style" is not necessarily kosher according to the dietary laws.

Wines

Check the requirements of the synagogue if you plan to serve wines. Some permit only certified kosher wines (including champagnes); others allow all wines. Liquors (scotch, rye, etc.) do not require certification.

PRACTICAL MATTERS

Your wedding may be one of the largest expenditures you make until you buy your first home. Think of it as a service you are buying, instead of the emotional high point of your life to date, and you and your family will be more easily able to make business-like decisions.

You may be debating lace tablecloths versus high fashion colors in linens, or dreaming of orchids floating in waterfalls as fantasy ideas in decoration, but your father will be signing a contract with the caterer which is an ironclad business deal. Approach the discussion with a clear budget in mind and a good approximation of the size of your guest list.

Any cancellation, changes, or last minute additions will cost additional money—usually large sums. There has probably never been an instance of a change in plans resulting in lower costs after a contract is negotiated! Even with a contract, you should be prepared for an inevitable cost overrun.

Insurance

Insurance is now available to cover the loss resulting from a cancellation or postponement forced by a drastic change in plans. For weddings booked long in advance of the date, it is a prudent measure. Ask whether the caterer supplies this service, or whether you must buy it independently. You should be covered for the loss of your deposit as well as for the loss of the entire fee. Check the conditions allowed for cancellation or changes in your plans. No one is immune to accident, illness, or other family emergencies. May you have a good policy—and never have to file a claim on it!

Basic Questions

Check the following at each place you visit and *write down the answers* in a notebook or on cards you carry along.

1. Will yours be the only wedding or will there be another function at that time?

2. If there are to be others, what provision will be made for the proper reception of your guests and privacy for the party?

3. What rooms are available and how will they be set up? Look. Is there a separate rental fee for the room? What services and equipment are included in

the fee? (Furnishings, tableware, candles, cake table and service, piano and dance floor, coat checking, bar setup, valet or free parking?) Check the rest rooms, too.

4. What choices are there in table settings and room appointments? Can we see samples?

5. What menus are offered? Cost of each? Will guests be offered a choice, or do we choose one set menu?

6. Are there choices of meal service (captain-served buffet, French, white glove, etc.)? Cost of each?

7. What planning assistance is offered (host, maître d', consultant)?

8. Who will provide

	Cost
florist for room deco- rations, bouquets	$_____
personalized items— *yarmulkes*, napkins and matches	_____
Grace booklets *(bent-shers)*	_____
individual menus	_____

Can you choose some, all, or none of these?

Cost

Can you provide them yourself?

9. Bar—On what basis is the bar figured?

   * open bar—how long?   _____

   wine waiter and bar cart during dinner   _____

   * open bar plus unlimited wine service during dinner   _____

   champagne and wine service only   _____

   cocktail bar, then bottles per table during dinner (including cordials)   _____

Can we specify the brands we want and have the caterer provide them?

What is the charge for setup and bar service if we provide our own liquor and wine?   _____

   * Price usually based on caterer's experience of average consumption per guest.

10. Cocktail hour

What foods will be served?

Compare: hot and cold hors d'oeuvres trays   _____

Cost

smorgasbord buf-
fet, captain-carved   _____

11. Nonalcoholic bever-
ages
    What will be offered?

12. *Hallah* and wedding
cake
    Is this included in the
cost? If not, what is the
charge?   _____
    Can we see samples
of the caterer's cake? Taste?
Can we provide our own
cake?

13. Desserts
    What desserts are on
the menu besides the wed-
ding cake?
    Is a Viennese table (a
lavish dessert buffet) offered? What is the extra
cost? What is served? What
happens to leftovers?   _____

14. Gratuities
    Who should be
tipped?
    Are these tips added
to the bill?
    If not, how much is
recommended and how and

Cost

when should these be paid
(cash or checks)?   _____

If coatroom and park-
ing tips are paid by the host,
will a "no tipping" sign be
posted?

15. Children (if you will
be inviting a number)

Is there a special chil-
dren's menu, children's
price? (They do not con-
sume liquor.)   _____

16. Liability

Is the caterer insured
for breakage, injury to
guests?

17. Music

Does the caterer rec-
ommend certain musicians?
Fees?   _____

Can you provide your
own? Must they be union
members?

Will they play for the
ceremony?

18. Price basis

Cost figured per per-
son   _____

per hour of bar and
buffet service   _____

"Package" rate   _____

Cost

what does the package include?

what will be extra?

Overtime charges

how many hours of service are included?

is there an overtime charge for extra hours? _____

for service after a certain hour?

when?

how much? _____

19. Other costs

Are there charges for

less than a minimum number of guests?

exceeding the final head count?

meals for the band (should not be charged as guest meals)

Cost-of-living charges? Guaranteed price for a future date?

At a synagogue

Is there a separate fee for the use of the sanctuary? _____

Does this include

(extra fee, if any)

the huppah _____

rabbi _____

Cost

cantor   _____

choir   or   other

music   _____   _____

(Total)

At a hotel

What setup is available for the ceremony?

Who will officiate? Check the ceremony details.

Is there a special room rate for out-of-town guests?

Is there a complimentary bridal suite?

For home catering service

Where will the food be prepared?

How will it be refrigerated till served?

Is there a delivery charge? For food? For rented equipment? For ice?

Will garbage be taken away after cleanup (important for a large party)?

Economizing

When you have described your wishes to the caterer and selected a menu and style that pleases you, you may find the price to be much more than you budgeted. After you have checked carefully to determine just what is included in the caterer's price, ask how you can economize. This is the point in the negotiations to mention the sum you had in mind and ask the caterer how he can work within that budget.

A change of day or hour may affect the price, so will the menu choice. Do not be intimidated by comments from the caterer on "elegance" or "once-in-a-lifetime" parties. And watch the "might-as-wells"—they have a way of mounting up astronomically unless you keep a firm grip on the items you order and their cost, and reject any services you do not want.

Regardless of the size and price of the function, it is the caterer's responsibility to make it as perfect as possible.

Comparison Shopping

You can start your search for the ideal caterer by recalling weddings you have been to recently and asking friends for suggestions. Visit the places you are considering, go through all the questions on pages 140–148 in your preliminary conferences (write down the answers) and, if you like a place, go back to see a wedding or formal dinner in progress, especially if you have never been to a party there. Also note whether the people you will be dealing with are courteous and responsive to your wishes.

Have the caterer put his preliminary estimate in writing and take detailed notes so that you can think the plan over, and compare your estimates and impressions before you commit yourself.

If you are considering a restaurant or a country club, it is a good idea to have dinner there on a Saturday or Sunday, when presumably they are setting forth their best, at their busiest. Check—how crowded are the public rooms? Will your party have adequate privacy and quiet if the rest of the place is full? What type of clientele does the place draw? What ambiance is projected by the physical setting and the quality of service? Carefully check the condition of the rest rooms as they are maintained on a busy evening.

Comparison Chart

Caterer	Menu	Special features:	Total price:
_____	_____	_____	$_____
		_____	

Phone		Disadvantages:	
_____		_____	
		_____	

Notes:

Caterer	Menu	Special features:	Total price:
_____	_____	_____	$_____
		_____	

Phone		Disadvantages:	
_____		_____	
		_____	

Notes:

Caterer   Menu   **Special features:**   Total price:
_____   _____ _____ $_____

           _____ _____

           _____

Phone   **Disadvantages:**

_____   _____

Notes:

_____

Caterer   Menu   **Special features:**   Total price:
_____   _____ _____ $_____

           _____ _____

           _____

Phone   **Disadvantages:**

_____   _____

Notes:

References

Before you make a final decision, it is sensible and perfectly proper to ask whether you may see the completed preparations for a reception just before that wedding takes place. (You do not, of course, actually attend the wedding.) If you are not familiar with the caterer's work, you may ask for references—the names of those who have used the facilities recently. You may also ask whether it would be possible to taste certain dishes.

What other professional services would the caterer recommend (florist, photographer, musician, and the like)? If you like the caterer's work, try to use the people he recommends. Things will probably go more smoothly when the professionals are accustomed to working with each other.

Summary of Business Details

Caterer   Person
Selected _____ Phone _____ Dealt with _____
Total price, including taxes, tips, and extra charges
    $_____
Terms of Payment
Deposit _____ Payable on _____ Refundable
    until _____
Additional payments _____ Due _____
Final payment due _____
How to be paid: _____ cash, _____ certified
    check, _____ credit card

Note: Try to arrange a large final payment for the date of the affair, so that you have some leverage if you are not satisfied with some aspects of the service. In general, the largest part of the sum due should not be paid too far in advance, if you are working more than three months ahead.

There will be some inevitable unexpected extras. Be prepared to take them with good humor if they are reasonable.

Deadlines

	Due Date
Finalizing menu	_____
Preliminary head count	_____
Final exact number (the "guarantee")	_____
Seating plan for dinner	_____

Signing the Contract

The contract is a legal document. Ask to take it home and study it before signing it. The contract should state:

1. Specifically, all foods selected, for example, specific vegetables; not "cheese," but "Jarlsberg" or "Brie"; cuts of beef, etc. Also, the number and kinds of hors d'oeuvres, the specific champagnes, wines, and liquors.

2. The hours of service (if the caterer is coming to your home, the time of arrival and departure).

3. Whether or not there can be a future price increase. Try to arrange a written limit, for example: "No

more than a 10 percent increase because of market conditions."

4. The rooms to be used, with notice to you to approve any change, should it become necessary.

5. All the service details you agreed upon after discussion.

6. Terms of payment.

7. A cancellation clause outlining refunds if some change of plans is necessary.

8. For a home wedding, that you keep all uneaten meals and leftover foods, properly packaged for refrigeration or freezing, and that all garbage and trash will be taken away at the end of the party.

Enter into your financial record at the back of this book the sums you are committed for, and the amount of cash or checks you will need to have on hand on the day of the wedding. Include the cash you think you will need to tip delivery people, drivers, and other help on the days immediately preceding the wedding and on the wedding day itself. And remember, banks are closed on Sunday!

ELEGANCE AND ECONOMY

A wedding at home or in a noncatered rented space can be both elegant and relatively economical. You can accomplish this by limiting your guest list to those who really know the bride and groom, and by combining some purchased foods or dishes prepared by a party cook with home specialties that can be made ahead. The bride's friends and relatives can each contribute their most spectacular dessert or best buffet dish for a memorable spread. You might even have a "cook-in" instead of a shower, some weeks before the wedding, when you and your friends prepare everything for storage in your freezer.

You contribute elegance by splurging on hiring the best help for the day, renting fine linen, silver, china, and glassware if you do not have enough of your own, serving good wines and champagne, and filling the house with many candles (a sign of rejoicing) and flowers (which can even be from friends' gardens). Music can be provided by gifted friends or records or tapes. You can rent professional audio equipment.

To retain your serenity as bride and mother of the bride, be sure to delegate responsibility for receiving guests at the door, overseeing the help and serving food and drink, running the sound system and cleaning up.

It will be a warm and original party. If you like organizing things your own way and have a suitable place for it, such a wedding may realize your very personal dream for this day without totally fracturing the family finances.

See the checklist on page 31.

THE FLORIST

Flowers add grace and beauty to any wedding. They can also be so expensive as to become a very large item in your budget, especially if you follow a florist's suggestions to put floral decorations everywhere, up to and including the coatrooms, the wedding limousine, and a special flower for the bride's garter belt (to surprise the groom, a florist's magazine unblushingly suggests).

Before you set up a floral plan, check with your synagogue. Some favor only very simple decorations and do not allow a floral *huppah,* in the interest of keeping the spiritual significance of the ceremony uppermost.

Reject any suggestions to rent synthetic flowers or a plastic arbor to use as a *huppah.* No matter how "lifelike," these are always tacky. Better to use just a few beautiful flowers and let them stand out as ornaments.

If you or your friends will be doing the flowers yourselves, from blooms purchased wholesale, be sure you are dealing with a florist who will guarantee the freshest delivery the day before, and that you have enough containers and an adequate cool space to store your completed arrangements.

Basics

Your own bouquet, matched in formality and style to your gown

Corsages for the mothers and grandmothers

Boutonnieres for the groom, fathers, and grandfathers

Floral arrangement for the platform *(bimah)*

Centerpieces for the bridal table and buffet table

Pleasant and Usual

Bridal attendants' flowers
Boutonnieres for ushers and best man
Garlands for *huppah* poles
Centerpieces for each table
Floral arrangement for the bride's home

Exotic (and Expensive) Extras

Entrance and reception room floral decorations, palms, fountains, etc.

Aisle decorations

Floral *huppah*

Outdoor lighting, ornamental plants, and fountains for a garden wedding

Consider ordering "breakaway" centerpieces that come apart into small bouquets for guests to take home. Tell your caterer how you want this gift to your guests handled (see page 23).

For a cheerful informal note, consider decorating with balloons, with one or two lovely and unusual blooms in a bud vase for each table, or using a single ribbon-decorated flower for each attendant.

Thank-you flowers sent to the parents the day after the wedding are a thoughtful and gracious gesture from an appreciative honeymoon couple.

References

Ask your friends, your caterer, or your synagogue for recommendations. Observe as you attend functions yourself and ask who has done the flowers, if you like them.

Ask the florist to give you the names of people whose weddings he has done recently and check with them. Were they satisfied? Was everything delivered as promised?

Try to work with flowers in season, which are usually less expensive. Ask to see samples of the work done. Look around in the shop itself. Is it neat? Attractive? Do you see good flowers in the cooler and on display? Are the people you talk to friendly, courteous, receptive to your ideas?

Have a preliminary proposal made in writing, or take notes. Consider your plan carefully before placing a firm order.

Florist Checklist

Name of florist _____ Phone _____
Address _____
Person dealt with _____

	Expense of	
---	Bride	Groom
Bride's bouquet color and type of flowers		
_____	_____	_____
style _____		
Mothers' flowers (for both mothers) color and type of flowers		
_____	_____	_____
style _____		
Wedding party Matron/Maid of honor	_____	
color _____		

	Expense of	
	Bride	*Groom*
style _____		
Bridesmaids		
number _____	_____	
color _____		
style _____		
Flower girls		
number _____	_____	
color _____		
style _____		
Boutonnieres		
Groom		_____
Best Man		_____
Fathers and grandfathers		_____
Ushers		
number _____		_____
Ceremony decorations		
Platform *(bimah)*	_____	
Other decorations	_____	
Huppah	_____	
Reception decorations		
Color scheme _____		
Bridal table	_____	
Buffet table	_____	
Centerpieces		
number _____		
at _____	_____	
Other room decorations		
_____		
_____		
Subtotals	_____	_____
Sales tax	_____	_____
Grand total	_____	_____
Deposit	_____	_____
Balance	_____	_____

How (cash, certified check, credit card) and when
to be paid? _____
Enter these figures in your expense record.

Note: Some of these items are traditionally paid for
by the bride, some by the groom. The costs are sometimes shared in other ways (see page 39). Be sure all
the parties understand this. You may want to have the
orders made out and signed separately and the bills
presented separately.

Preserving Your Bouquet

Some florists are equipped to preserve and mount
your wedding flowers in a glass dome or a framed arrangement. Discuss this when you select your flowers,
as some dry better than others. There are also many
kits and books on the market that show you how to do
this yourself. You could mount a small garland of the
dried flowers arranged around your wedding invitation for an interesting keepsake.

THE MUSICIANS

Music is a very important part of any wedding, both
to enhance the ceremony and to lend the necessary
note of jubilation at the reception. When you have a
choice of musicians, seek recommendations from
friends and relatives and the caterer. Ask also what
music the synagogue or chapel can provide for the ceremony. Is there an organ? A choir?

Make time to audition the bands at work. Some will

offer you audition tapes as well. Does the sound at the live party equal what you hear on the tape? How do the musicians dress and behave at work? What types of music do they play? What ambiance do they project? Will they be able to play for the ceremony, if needed, as well as for the reception? What special features do they offer as entertainment? Will the bandleader serve as master of ceremonies? What do you think of his choice of humorous material? Do they have everyone up and dancing at the party you observe? Will they play your requests, including ethnic material? (See page 21 for notes on appropriate music for a Jewish wedding.)

Your choice can range from an instrumental soloist or a classical trio for a small reception to a full-size dance orchestra for a large one. Continuous music costs more, but it is worth it for the added liveliness it brings. So are strolling musicians during dinner. You will need three or four pieces for up to a hundred guests and five or six for a larger group. Some musicians base the required size of the band on the size of the reception hall.

Very popular musicians are often booked up well in advance, so start listening and looking early.

Details of the Musicians' Contract

Your contract should specify:

1. The number of players (the leader may count as two in some union contracts).

2. The fee per player.

3. The exact number of hours the musicians will play for this fee (allowing a half hour for setup).

4. Overtime charges (including the hour when overtime begins and the minimum charge).

5. Taxes and surcharges (In most states, music is not taxable. A surcharge for the union pension and welfare fund is legitimately added, often quoted as a percentage of the total price.)

6. Terms of payment

Total cost $_____

Deposit   _____

Balance due _____

(payable on the day of the wedding, not before) Enter the figures in your expense record at the back of this book.

7. Cancellation clause

Musicians Selected—Name of band_____

Leader_____ Phone_____

THE PHOTOGRAPHER

Your wedding pictures are a precious record. Hiring the best professional photographer you can afford will insure you against the disappointment and regret that come from poor pictures.

Relying on a camera-bug friend as your only photographer is not wise unless special circumstances make it difficult to hire a professional. It is an imposition on a guest, who may feel that the pressure to get perfect pictures spoils his enjoyment of the party. Moreover, as many a bride has discovered to her regret, champagne and cameras do not mix well.

To select a photographer, get recommendations from friends and the caterer. Look through your friends' albums and visit several studios. Examine the work carefully. Do you see the kind of pictures you would like for yourself? Is the person you speak with courteous and responsive to your ideas, or does he or she seem to have only one standard set of photos in mind?

Planning the Picture-taking

Plan with the photographer just what photos you want included, and which are to be taken before the ceremony (when everyone is freshest), and which just after the reception. How many family shots do you want? Do you want a photo of each table with the bride and groom? If there will be candid photos, which events and which members of the family and which friends do you want to concentrate on?

Whether your synagogue allows it or not (most do not), do not permit picture-taking during the ceremony. You do not want the solemnity of the wedding ritual marred by an obtrusive photographer bobbing up and down the aisle, popping flashbulbs in guests' eyes. Shots of the ceremony can be posed right after the recessional. When photos are allowed, have your photographer catch people in the procession just before they step into the doorway. Telephoto and "zoom" lenses can also be used by a skillful photographer to get candid shots of the ceremony without interrupting the ritual.

Formal Wedding Portraits

Though you can arrange to be photographed in your gown at the time of the final fitting, so that you have a bridal photo for newspaper announcements, most brides wisely wait until the wedding day for this picture. There is a deep feeling against actually wearing the wedding dress before the day and, as everyone knows, you will look your best in the special radiance of the wedding day. You can use your engagement photo or any other portrait you like for news releases.

Videotaping and Movies

If you want a professional videotape or movie of your wedding, ask for the use of two cameras, one battery-operated and portable, allowing for a variety of angles, tape that can be edited, and special effects such as fadeouts, zoom-ins, and vignettes.

Before ordering this, ask yourself whether you really want to watch your wedding on TV or home movies, or would you rather just have photos you can share and enjoy without gadgetry.

If you do have friends who offer to tape or film your wedding, remind them that you expect them to be unobtrusive and to keep out of the way of the professional still photographer.

Details of the Photographer's Contract

1. Will the photographer who made the samples you've seen be the same one who photographs your wedding?

2. Get a firm price for the photo albums, specifying the number of pages and the cost of additional pictures and additional albums of varying sizes.

3. Specify the number of pictures to be taken at the wedding and the number of proofs to be shown you.

4. Specify that you will choose the pictures to be included in the finished work.

5. Specify the time when the photographer will arrive, allowing enough time before the ceremony for the pictures you want, and the time when he will leave. Specify that he is to be properly dressed.

6. Can you save by having slides made and ordering only those prints you want to exhibit or share?

7. Can you keep the negatives? (They are usually thrown out.)

8. The contract should include:

   a cancellation clause

   exact prices for each size picture $_____

   specific parts of any "package deal"

   exact time, date, and place of the affair and hours for the photographer _____

   actual number of photos and

albums ordered, including
pages per album _____ @

_____   _____

number of pictures to be taken
and proofs given to you

_____

                              Total price   _____

Terms of payment:
    deposit _____ due _____
    * balance _____ due _____
    * should be on delivery of
      satisfactory work

Enter the money figures in your expense record at
the back of this book.

Photographer selected _____
Address _____
Phone _____
Name of person dealt with _____

TRANSPORTATION

Coordinate your need for cars and drivers. If you
will be hiring limousines, be sure the drivers have the
correct addresses and times for their pickups, as well
as their destinations. If the reception will be at a different location from the ceremony, be sure your car
pool drivers also know the address and, above all, how
to get there. Give the drivers a list of their passengers.

Arrange for payment of hired drivers either before
or after the wedding. You tip a hired driver, but not
the owner of a livery car.

Bride and Parents

Driver _____ Phone _____
Time to be at house _____ Transfer to reception* _____
Fee _____

Groom and Parents

Driver _____ Phone _____
Time to be at house _____ Transfer to reception* _____
Fee _____
(Allow an hour for photos and so on before the ceremony.)

* For the trip to the reception, the bride and groom ride together while the parents may share the car used to transport the groom and his parents.

Bridesmaids (to ceremony and transfer to reception)

Name _____ Driver _____ Phone _____
_____ _____ _____
_____ _____ _____
_____ _____ _____
_____ _____ _____
_____ _____ _____
Time to be at house* _____

* Allow enough time for them to arrive at the synagogue or hall from their homes a half hour before the ceremony, at least, earlier if they are to dress together.

Car Pool (for guests who may need a ride from one location to the other)

Driver _____ Passengers _____

_____

Driver _____ Passengers _____

_____

Driver _____ Passengers _____

_____

Note: If you will be meeting planes or trains for out-of-town guests, compile a similar list for their transportation. Don't attempt to have any member of the wedding party carry out this chore on the wedding day. Possible traffic jams on the way to the ceremony are enough to contend with on this day!

XIX

COUNTDOWN TO THE WEDDING DAY

AS SOON AS YOUR ENGAGEMENT IS ANNOUNCED

1. Set the wedding date (check dates when weddings may not be held, page 25).

2. Decide, in conference with both families, on the wedding style for you.

3. Start work on your guest list and the groom's list. Make a preliminary head count.

4. Make a reservation at your synagogue, or begin to look for a caterer and a pleasing location for the ceremony and reception.

5. Attend weddings and other functions with a "shopper's eye."

6. Don't delay meeting with your rabbi if there are possible problems from a previous divorce or a difference of religion.

7. Go house or apartment hunting with your fiancé. Set aside days for furniture shopping.

THREE MONTHS BEFORE THE WEDDING (or as soon as you can for a less formal, quickly arranged affair)

1. Reserve the location and the caterer. Set dates for planning conferences before the wedding.

2. Shop for your gown and veil and your mother's dress and accessories. Allow at least six weeks for the delivery of custom-made clothes.

3. Name your maid or matron of honor and bridesmaids. Remind your fiancé to choose his ushers and best man.

4. If the wedding will be held at home, start work on the garden, house refurbishing, and cleaning.

5. Visit photographers and florists; audition musicians. Engage each one as soon as you can. Set dates for conferences with each at least three weeks before the wedding.

6. Confer with your attendants to decide on the best price range for their dresses. Select the outfits you would like them to wear. Don't go shopping with more than one bridesmaid if you want to avoid confusion and conflict.

7. With your fiancé, select your china, silver, crystal, and linen patterns. List your choices and your bridal registries in your file for friends who ask.

8. Finalize your guest list. Give the groom's family a style sample for writing up their list and a deadline date for delivery of the list to you. Write up your own master list (see pages 45–48).

9. Order your invitations, the number to total a few more than your guest list to allow for errors in addressing. Also order your imprinted formal and informal notepaper and return address labels or embosser.

TWO MONTHS BEFORE THE WEDDING

1. Pick up your envelopes from the stationer so you can start addressing them. Do you have your fiancé's list?

2. Buy your wedding shoes and lingerie before the fitting for your wedding gown. Arrange to have shoes dyed.

3. Tell your attendants what store and which dresses you have chosen. Make a date for them to go together to order them. The matron or maid of honor should help you by keeping track of these appointments.

4. Ask the bridesmaids to meet to shop for shoes and have them all dyed together. Buy gloves if they are to be worn. Select a proper shade of hose and have

them delivered with the dresses, including an extra pair or two for emergencies.

5. As soon as your mother decides on the color and style of her ensemble, describe it to the groom's mother (dress and sleeve length, head covering, degree of formality). Suggest several colors among which she may choose to harmonize with the overall color scheme.

6. Shop for your wedding day gift to your new husband.

SIX WEEKS BEFORE THE WEDDING

1. Pick up your invitations. Finish addressing, seal and stamp the sets, and mail them out.

2. Notify bridesmaids to go for their fittings when their dresses arrive.

3. Have your own fitting, wearing the shoes and underthings you will use on the wedding day.

4. Make appointments for physical and dental checkups.

5. Has the groom selected his best man and ushers and arranged for their outfits?

6. With your fiancé, select your wedding ring or rings, and order the engraving. (Groom's initials/to/ bride's initials/date; reverse the order for the groom's ring.)

7. Select gifts for bridesmaids. Remind the groom to select gifts for his party.

8. Buy insurance for your new home and a floater to cover your wedding gifts.

9. If you are going to change your name, start now on the notifications (see page 100).

10. Attend to other personal business details (see Chapter XI).

11. Start preparing for your wedding trip. Check your reservations and transportation (usually the groom's responsibility), luggage, wardrobe, and the like.

12. Make an appointment to confer with the rabbi, if you have not seen him before.

FOUR WEEKS BEFORE THE WEDDING

1. Check off your responses as they come in. File the reply cards, if you are using them.

2. Plan housing for out-of-town attendants and guests. Do they need transportation from the airport or station? Will you have to entertain them before or after the reception? Make arrangements now.

3. Engage special traffic police or parking attendants if you will need them at your reception.

4. Arrange for your blood test. Remind the groom to get his. Coordinate this appointment to comply with marriage license requirements in your state.

5. Arrange your "ladies' luncheon" or dinner for the attendants, perhaps at the same time as the bachelor dinner. This is the occasion to give the attendants their gifts.

6. Your prewedding social engagements will be filling your calendar. Keep a careful record and give a schedule to your mother, your fiancé, and those attendants who are also invited.

7. Give the musicians any special music you want them to prepare.

8. Continue working on the personal business details in Chapter XI.

9. Confer with the florist and photographer you have engaged.

TWO WEEKS BEFORE THE WEDDING

1. Make your hair and manicure appointments. For a real bit of *luxe,* have the hairdresser come to your home on your wedding day to arrange your hair after you dress.

2. Make a date with your fiancé to get your marriage license. Don't be upset if it turns out to be a tension-filled hour! It always is. To relax, go out afterward for lunch or cocktails together and toast your forthcoming wedding.

3. Select a special outfit to wear to your fiancé's *oyfruf* (see page 74). Dress as for holiday synagogue

attendance. Check whether your mother and father will need hats.

4. Invite relatives and friends to the *oyfruf*. Informal notes or phone calls are fine.

5. Check all your suppliers and services to be sure everything is going along as scheduled.

6. Address and assemble your announcements, if you will be using them. Entrust them to your mother or a friend to mail the day *after* the wedding, not before.

7. Send out your newspaper announcements in accordance with publication deadlines (see Chapter XIII).

8. Make up your seating plan for the dinner.

9. Make up a request list for the musicians.

10. Give the rabbi the names of those to be honored at the *oyfruf* (see page 65).

THE LAST WEEK BEFORE THE WEDDING

Now, when you want to run, is the time to slow down a bit. Do it by organizing things carefully, taking the time to eat properly, and getting to bed early as many evenings as you can.

1. Count up your acceptances. As the deadline approaches, you may call those who have been thoughtless enough not to respond. But do not count in any

"maybes" or "no responses." Your caterer should be able to handle a few extra guests, and a few "no-shows," unfortunately, will always be with us. Give the caterer your final count and forget about it. You have hired the caterer to worry for you.

2. Assemble in one place all the things you need to dress for the wedding: underthings, hose, gown, veil, shoes and cosmetics. Fill your little personal handbag for the day. Wrap your gift for your bridegroom and put it with this bag. Don't leave anything for last minute scurrying about.

3. Pack the suitcases and your travel handbag for the wedding trip. Are your reservations made? Transportation set?

4. Make up an emergency kit for your wedding day: safety pins, bobby pins, Band-Aids, tissues, needle and thread, aspirins.

5. Estimate how much time you will need for each step in dressing on the wedding day. Then set up a time chart that will allow you to do everything slowly, so that you *appear* calm. Eventually, the slow motion will make you *feel* calm as well.

6. Gather up some sheets of tissue paper or a clean sheet to spread in the car for the ride to the ceremony. Try to arrange the skirt of your dress so that you do not sit on it. If there is a train, spread it on the back of the car seat.

7. Stay with a "natural" makeup and apply it carefully, since it must last for hours. Blotting and powdering between applications of lipstick make it more permanent. Be sure your mascara and eyeliner

are waterproof and smudgeproof. Brides, like Miss America, often cry for joy. And don't forget your deodorant.

8. Everything is in order. All the planning you've done is coming to bear now, as all the details are being taken care of by other hands. Relax. Step out on your right foot and enjoy this happy day.

MAZAL TOV AND SIMAN TOV!

A Happy Wedding and a Bright Future to You Both!

AFTER THE WEDDING

The happy couple have left. But you, the mother of the bride, still have a few pleasant duties, and the activity will probably be welcome to stave off the "postparty blues."

1. You will have to entertain your out-of-town guests after an afternoon reception. An informal supper for them and the wedding party is a pleasant way of winding down.

2. Pack up and freeze the top layer of the wedding cake for the bride and groom's first anniversary.

3. Have the wedding gown professionally cleaned and packed to preserve it.

4. You may want to arrange for the preservation of the bridal bouquet.

5. Mail out the wedding announcements the day after the wedding.

6. Acknowledge any telegrams that have been sent to you. Save the ones sent to the bride and groom for them to answer.

7. Keep track of gifts sent in after the wedding.

A considerate bride and groom will call their parents when they arrive at their honeymoon destination to let them know that all is well, and thank them for the splendid wedding they have given their children.

A Special Gift—Hakhnasat Kallah

The day may come when you will no longer want to keep your bridal outfit on the top shelf of the closet. You can accomplish a unique act of charity *(Tzedakah)* and a special *mitzvah,* that of helping the bride rejoice *(Hakhnasat Kallah),* by giving your bridal gown, veil, and headdress to a Jewish organization that will lend them to poor brides. The finery you no longer need will enhance the rejoicing of other young women who cannot buy lovely gowns for their special day.

The gowns you send to the organizations below will not be sold, but lent more than once to many young brides.

Where to Donate Bridal Gowns, Bridesmaids' and Mothers' Dresses

Note: Before mailing, call or write to confirm that gowns are still needed, to check the mailing address, and to find out whether a courier might be available to take the package to Israel. Dresses should have long sleeves and high necks, though you might inquire if in doubt about a décolletage.

In the United States

For use in Neve Yerushalayim Yeshiva for girls, write:

> Evelyn Seitzman
> 161–55 Jewel Avenue
> Flushing, N.Y. 11365

For use in New York by N'shei Ahavas Chesed (Women's League for Community Services) call:

> Blimi Glustein, 212/851-1812, or write
> Women's League for Community Services
> 1680 47th Street
> Brooklyn, N.Y. 11204

In Israel

> Daniel Kuttler Charity Fund
> Karen Hayesod Street 7
> Jerusalem, Israel

> Rabbanit Bracha Kapach
> 12 Lod Street
> Jerusalem, Israel

To mail, mark package "USED CLOTHES"; maximum weight—twenty-two pounds.

This is a project you might want to initiate in your sisterhood if you live outside of the metropolitan area.

NOTES

XX

WHEN YOU HAVE TO CHANGE YOUR PLANS

Let us hope you will never have to use this section. But the best-intentioned people in the world sometimes come to the conclusion that a planned wedding should not take place. And there are times when events beyond your control can force a change in already announced arrangements. There are set procedures that can help you over these difficult hurdles and lessen the strain and embarrassment for all.

WHEN AN ENGAGEMENT IS BROKEN

A couple who decide to break their engagement and call off their wedding plans must first of all inform their parents, who can then go ahead with the necessary business of canceling contracts, if they have already been set, and recalling any invitations that have been sent out.

Recalling invitations

If the wedding will not take place, guests who have already been invited must be notified at once. This may be by phone, handwritten notes, telegram, or if there is time, printed cards. The card may read:

> *Mr. and Mrs. Walter Stern*
> *announce that the marriage of their daughter*
> *Cynthia*
> *to*
> *Mr. Robert Harris*
> *will not take place*

No reason need be given. A handwritten note could follow the same form.

If the recall must be made by phone, assign a few friends or relatives of your mother, who being less emotionally involved, can take the necessary formal but cordial tone and keep conversation at a minimum. All the caller need say is, perhaps, "This is Alice Taylor, Mrs. Stern's sister. She has asked me to call you and tell you that her daughter Cynthia's wedding, which was to take place next Sunday, has been canceled." Again, no reason need be given.

Newspaper announcements

If a formal announcement has been sent to the newspapers, the family may wish to announce the end of the engagement, but it is not always done. Lovers' quarrels are often patched up as spontaneously as they first occurred. If the family feels that an announcement is necessary, the briefest statement is enough:

Mr. and Mrs. Walter Stern of Fairfield, Connecticut announce that the engagement of their daughter Cynthia to Mr. Robert Harris has been broken by mutual consent.

Engagement presents

To whom does the engagement ring belong? Legally, the woman may keep it, but she usually offers to return it. If her ex-fiancé insists that she keep it, she may wear it, but not, of course, on the ring finger.

Any other gifts from him, his family, or friends, belong to her and need not be returned, though many women do return them to make their decision final.

Wedding presents

All wedding presents sent to the bride before the wedding must be returned to the senders, with a brief note, stating simply that the wedding will not take place, and thanking the senders for their thoughtful generosity.

WHEN THERE IS A DEATH IN THE FAMILY

Once the date has been set for a wedding, it need not be called off even if there has been a death in the immediate family. Indeed, in Orthodox tradition, it *must* not be called off. A wedding is considered such a mitzvah that even mourning may be interrupted to permit it to take place.

In such circumstances, though, the family may want to have a very quiet wedding, canceling the music for example, and having only a small family reception instead of the lavish affair originally planned. This may require the recall of invitations already mailed out.

If time permits, a card may be printed reading:

> *Mr. and Mrs. Walter Stern*
> *regret that because of a death in the family*
> *the invitations to their daughter's wedding*
> *on Sunday, March twelfth*
> *must be recalled*

If the time is too short, guests may be notified by phone or by written notes.

If the wedding date falls after the formal mourning period, but less than a year after the death, and you want to go ahead with your plans, you can resolve any doubts and questions about the propriety of the reception by discussing it with the rabbi who will officiate. He will be able to tell you what modifications, if any, you must make.

APPENDIX

YOUR EXPENSE RECORD

This is your cash flow, or what-is-it-all-going-to-cost page. Enter all your firm commitments here as soon as they are made. This will give you a quick overview of your budget, your cash and check needs, and insure that you do not forget an expense item you have contracted for ahead of time. Due dates are kept track of here, too.

	Totals	Charge/ Check	Cash

Synagogue
Name/address

_____

_____

Phone _____

Person to contact

_____

Fee $_____

Deposit $_____

	Totals	Charge/ Check	Cash

Balance $_____   _____

Caterer
Name/address
_____
_____
_____
Phone _____
Total contract
  $_____
Payments due/date
  $_____
  _____   _____

Musicians
Name/address
_____
_____
_____
Phone _____
Fee $_____
Deposit $_____
Balance $_____   _____

Photographer
Name/address
_____
_____
_____
Phone _____
Total contract
  $_____
Proof date _____
Delivery date
  _____
Deposit $_____
Balance $_____   _____

	Totals	Charge/ Check	Cash

Stationer
Name/address

_____

_____

Phone _____
Total order
$_____
Delivery/pickup date

_____

Deposit $_____
Balance $_____   _____

Florist
Name/address

_____

_____

Phone _____
  Bridal flowers
   $_____
  Decorations

   _____

  Other flowers

   _____

  Total order
   $_____
Deposit $_____
Balance:
  bride $_____
  groom $_____
Delivery tips
  $_____   _____

Clothes
Bridal gown
  $_____

	Totals	Charge/ Check	Cash

Veil $_____

Shoes $_____

  Shop _____

  _____

  Fitter _____

  Phone _____

  Deposit

    $_____

  Balance

    $_____   _____

Bridesmaids

  Shop _____

  _____

  Fitter _____

  Phone _____

Items you will be paying for:

  hose, accessories, etc.   _____

Gifts to bridesmaids   _____

Mother's gown

  Shop _____

  _____

  Fitter _____

  Phone _____

  Deposit

    $_____

  Balance

    $_____   _____

Miscellaneous

Yarmulkes

  color _____

  # _____

  @ _____

  Supplier _____

  _____

	Totals	Charge/ Check	Cash
Phone _____	_____		__

Grace booklets
  # _____
  @ _____
  Supplier _____
  _____

Phone _____   _____

Other reception items (list)

_____   _____
_____   _____
_____   _____

  Supplier _____
  _____

  Phone _____   _____

Rental Items (for home or
  self-catered weddings)
List:

_____   _____
_____   _____
_____   _____

Supplier _____
_____

Phone _____
Delivery date
  _____

Deposit $_____
Balance $_____
Tips $_____   _____

Total Cash Needed for Tips
  $_____

            Grand Totals   _____

Panic-stopper

Make separate lists of all these names and phone numbers on cards for yourself and your mother. Give the groom's mother and the groom a card with only those numbers they will need, such as the florist and the drivers. They should not call any of the other suppliers you will be dealing with, but clear their requests through you or your mother.

A NOTE FOR THE NON-JEWISH GUEST

The key to this occasion is the injunction to rejoice. Dress up for the occasion. Wear the most elaborate outfit suitable to the time of the day. Women may need some head covering in the sanctuary, if the ceremony will be held in a synagogue. Afterward at the reception, they should follow the lead of the hostess.

If skullcaps will be worn by the men, the host will give you one. Wear it in the sanctuary. At the dinner afterward, follow the lead of the other men.

Forget all about your diet for the day. The reception, to which, with very rare exceptions, all are invited, includes lavish food and drink. If you have been invited to a reception before the ceremony, come a bit early, ready to partake of a generous buffet.

Above all, enjoy, enjoy! You have been invited to help the bride and groom rejoice.

About the *oyfruf*: If you have been invited to the *oyfruf*, you will be attending Sabbath services. Dress as for church attendance, remembering that men and married women will need a head covering, that you do not drive up to the door of an Orthodox synagogue, and you do not carry packages, briefcases, newspapers, umbrellas, and large, bulging handbags to any synagogue. When in doubt, ask your host.

Come prepared to participate in the rejoicing and a fine reception *(kiddush)* afterward.

CALENDAR

Our wedding day is _____ .

              (month)   (date)

The TWELFTH WEEK before our wedding is the week of

_____ .

(month)   (date)

	Morning	*Afternoon*	*Evening*
SUNDAY			
MONDAY			
TUESDAY			
WEDNESDAY			
THURSDAY			
FRIDAY			
SATURDAY			

Our wedding day is _____ .
                    (month)   (date)

The ELEVENTH WEEK before our wedding is the week of
_____ .
(month)   (date)

	Morning	*Afternoon*	*Evening*
SUNDAY			
MONDAY			
TUESDAY			
WEDNESDAY			
THURSDAY			
FRIDAY			
SATURDAY			

Our wedding day is _____.
                    (month)   (date)

The TENTH WEEK before our wedding is the week of

_____.
(month)   (date)

	Morning	Afternoon	Evening
SUNDAY			
MONDAY			
TUESDAY			
WEDNESDAY			
THURSDAY			
FRIDAY			
SATURDAY			

Our wedding day is _____.
               (month)   (date)

The NINTH WEEK before our wedding is the week of
_____.
(month)   (date)

	Morning	*Afternoon*	*Evening*
SUNDAY			
MONDAY			
TUESDAY			
WEDNESDAY			
THURSDAY			
FRIDAY			
SATURDAY			

Our wedding day is _____.
(month) (date)

The EIGHTH WEEK before our wedding is the week of
_____.
(month) (date)

	Morning	Afternoon	Evening
SUNDAY			
MONDAY			
TUESDAY			
WEDNESDAY			
THURSDAY			
FRIDAY			
SATURDAY			

Our wedding day is _____ .
　　　　　　　　　(month)　　　　　　　　　　　　(date)

The SEVENTH WEEK before our wedding is the week of
_____ .
(month)　　　　　　　　　　(date)

	Morning	Afternoon	Evening
SUNDAY			
MONDAY			
TUESDAY			
WEDNESDAY			
THURSDAY			
FRIDAY			
SATURDAY			

Our wedding day is _____.
                    (month)   (date)

The SIXTH WEEK before our wedding is the week of
_____.
(month)   (date)

	Morning	*Afternoon*	*Evening*
SUNDAY			
MONDAY			
TUESDAY			
WEDNESDAY			
THURSDAY			
FRIDAY			
SATURDAY			

Our wedding day is _____.
                  (month)   (date)

The FIFTH WEEK before our wedding is the week of
_____.
(month)   (date)

	Morning	*Afternoon*	*Evening*
SUNDAY			
MONDAY			
TUESDAY			
WEDNESDAY			
THURSDAY			
FRIDAY			
SATURDAY			

Our wedding day is _____ .
               (month)   (date)

The FOURTH WEEK before our wedding is the week of

_____ .
(month)   (date)

	Morning	*Afternoon*	*Evening*
SUNDAY			
MONDAY			
TUESDAY			
WEDNESDAY			
THURSDAY			
FRIDAY			
SATURDAY			

Our wedding day is _____ .
              (month)   (date)

The THIRD WEEK before our wedding is the week of
_____ .
(month)   (date)

	Morning	*Afternoon*	*Evening*
SUNDAY			
MONDAY			
TUESDAY			
WEDNESDAY			
THURSDAY			
FRIDAY			
SATURDAY			

Our wedding day is _____.
                      (month)   (date)

The SECOND WEEK before our wedding is the week of
_____.
(month)   (date)

	Morning	*Afternoon*	*Evening*
SUNDAY			
MONDAY			
TUESDAY			
WEDNESDAY			
THURSDAY			
FRIDAY			
SATURDAY			

Our wedding day is _____.
            (month)   (date)

The LAST WEEK before our wedding is the week of
_____.
(month)   (date)

	Morning	*Afternoon*	*Evening*
SUNDAY			
MONDAY			
TUESDAY			
WEDNESDAY			
THURSDAY			
FRIDAY			
SATURDAY			

NOTES